Confessions of a Boat Lover's Wife or

Is a Marriage Like This Worth Saving?

Confessions of a Boat Lover's Wife
or
Is a Marriage Like This Worth Saving?

Mina Bess Lewis
Introduction by John R. Whiting

Hearst Marine Books   New York

Copyright © 1987 by Mina Bess Lewis

All rights reserved. No part of this book may be reproduced or utilized in any form or by any means, electronic or mechanical, including photocopying, recording or by any information storage and retrieval system, without permission in writing from the Publisher. Inquiries should be addressed to Permissions Department, William Morrow and Company, Inc., 105 Madison Ave., New York, N.Y. 10016.

Library of Congress Cataloging-in-Publication Data

Lewis, Mina Bess.
  Confessions of a boat lover's wife, or, Is a marriage like this worth saving?

    1. Boats and boating—Anecdotes, facetiae, satire, etc.   2. Lewis, Mina Bess.   I. Title.   II. Title: Is a marriage like this worth saving?
GV777.3.L48   1987   797.1′092′4   86-18438
ISBN 0-688-06918-5

Printed in the United States of America

First Edition

1 2 3 4 5 6 7 8 9 10

BOOK DESIGN BY PATRICE FODERO

*To Myra Doniger,
Marlo Lewis, Jr.,
and the Captain who
steered a safe course for us all*

Acknowledgments

My thanks to Chapman's *Piloting, Seamanship & Small Boat Handling* for answering a thousand and one questions. To the Power Squadron for forewarning, forearming, and forestalling. To the Coast Guard for just being there. To Lucille Ball, Liam O'Brien, Jennings Lang, Hal Wallis, Roberta Peters, Alex Gottlieb, and Marge Jacobs for their enthusiasm and encouragement. To John Whiting for his urbane understanding. To Sarah Borden for her cheering attention.

—Mina Bess Lewis

Preface

The clash upon the sea, between the sexes, which Mina Bess Lewis writes about so deftly in these pages, goes back more than decades, more than centuries—actually millennia. Cleopatra herself commanded ships upon the Nile and did it so spectacularly that in the early nineteenth century a famous and luxurious American yacht was named *Cleopatra's Barge*. It wasn't a coal barge!

Since Cleopatra that battle has been seesawing. As late as the middle of the twentieth century, when our author was beginning her seagoing career, your standard yacht club could be accused of thinking about itself as an institution for men only. Of course ladies were honored guests on Great Occasions. Even the New York Yacht Club, not so average, showed its true colors by having a very small list of "lady associate members." And the United States Power Squadrons (with four hundred squadrons all across the country) chose its members with care, ostensibly to combine seagoing knowledge and companionability at the meetings. By coincidence, all the members were men. Ah! This was to change, as we shall see.

The other war, between boat owners and those who provide goods and services, was often pretty hot too in those olden days. Dealers, yacht brokers, marina operators, chandlers, boatyards—Mina Bess knows them all. Her hand, with its figurative pen, is more deft than that of Jack London. His autobiographical tussle of three quarters of a century ago, called "Sharks in the Boatyard," doesn't really have a smile in it. Just a gritting of teeth. Mrs. Lewis has a softer, more humorous touch.

Oh, there has been a great sea change, with family outboards racing up and down the inland lakes and rivers as well as across the saltwater bays. Those who go down to the sea to make a buck now look to sell that family market, so they know it's best to hide—indeed, to overcome—their sharklike features. The people who race boats across the waves—oceangoing sailboats or thundering offshore power boats, have discovered that women have a place aboard. That place may be at the wheel of a hot twin-motor rig. It certainly is a more comfortable place than the overnight duty station of my good friend Marion Van Sant, who was said to have liked sailboat racing so much that she was willing to crouch in the forepeak to give a little ballast forward. Big races in the eighties have women handling sails, navigating, and *working*. (As family members aboard boats, they had been working all along, of course.) Moreover, the New York Yacht Club has women members serving on committees. The Power Squadrons changed their ways, in the end quite gracefully, and now accept women members.

It's noticeable everywhere.

I have recently seen a delicately plump lady in a purple bathing suit sailing a Windsurfer in the Block Island Salt Pond—and when I looked again I realized she was pregnant.

I've seen women sailing their own boats in top races, of course. Queene Hooper's *Moonfleet* kept moving nicely in the hot competition of the Newport-Bermuda Race. She hasn't won the race yet, but neither have a couple of hundred male skippers.

Some things are gone, no doubt—like the joshing of those bygone days, when boats were not called "it" like an automobile, but "she." Imagine the days when the *Charles W. Morgan* or *Dreadnaught* or the *Joseph Conrad* was called "she." This was really an honor, of course, to both the ship and the fair sex. Ah, well! It used to be considered clever to note that a craft with a trim and well-tucked stern had "good buttocks," or that a boat in a storm was "breasting the waves." But nowadays it is no longer fashionable for men to go down to the sea in clichés, and this has caused just as much of an improvement in the language as in the courtesies.

So there you have me noting a serious meaning in the writings of Mina Bess Lewis. She is not just Erma Bombeck trying to go motorboating and sailing on Lake Wobegon. She is a chronicler of the Meaningful Decades of Boating History—the period when yachting for the Elite Males gave way to millions of happy little boats.

There is perhaps a downside. Think of how boat names have changed. Once they honored famous women. Goddesses and queens, classical heroines and of course favorite daughters. But now, plastered in gold letters on the rear ends of cruisers, you can see *Mama's Mink,* or *John's Other Wife,* or even *Nox Vomica.*

When it comes to naming boats, there is more to it than splashing a bottle of champagne against the bow and saying "I christen thee *Elfleda.*" Part of the trick is to remember the dinghy, that miniature personal water taxi that is often towed astern. Someone should go down in history for naming a small rowboat *Tender Behind,* or *Trailing Arbutus.* What with all the high-speed slaloms cutting across the water, you are sure to see a dinghy named *Aprés-Ski*. As for *Elfleda's* dinghy . . . how about *Elf*?

Short names for boats are in. One family liked a familiar chart abbreviation, and now we have *Qk Fl Rd*. (That stands for Quick Flashing Red, a type of lighted buoy, of course.) As of this writing, I know of no one who has gone so much to the brief as to name a boat *Ms*. This is indeed a fortunate nonoccurrence.

Mina Bess Lewis, not being that particular kind of Constant Warrior, has not come up with a proposal to rename one of our mutually favorite books in nonsexist terms Chapperson's *Piloting, Seapersonship & Small Boat Handling*.

The deft rapier of her wit would never be used for that unkindest cut of all!

—JOHN WHITING
Block Island, R.I.

The Log

	Preface	9
	Pro Log	15
1.	Mac the Knife	17
2.	Schooldays, Schooldays...	23
3.	The Name of the Dame	29
4.	Anchors Can Be a Drag	35
5.	Phone Conversation Piece	41
6.	Special Delivery	45
7.	Weigh Off Broadway	53
8.	The Captain Flips	65
9.	Music Lovers, Arise	73
10.	Sinking in the Rain	79
11.	Bali Hi—and Belly Up	87
12.	Swede-Hearts No More	101
13.	Love Is Never Having to Say He's Wrong	107
14.	Don't Look Now, *Marlyn*, But You've Got a Hole in Your Bottom	119
15.	The Family That Sails Together...	125
16.	The Sea Is Full of Surprises	135
17.	Status Afflatus	141
18.	Before You Jump Off the Deep End	149
.	Epi Log	155

Pro Log

Each year when the hounds of spring are on winter's traces and the first flowers test the waking earth . . . when a vagrant breeze gives promise of lazy summer days in a garden sweet with bloom . . . then it is that I must go down to the sea again.

What is the reason? The tang of salt on a sun-drenched deck? The quiet of boundless space—or a far horizon stretching to adventure? Or is it the sea herself, ancient mother of us all, calling us to be rocked once more in that primeval cradle of life?

The hell it is! It's because I'm married to a nut, that's why. A boat nut. One of an eccentric species unlike any other. An obsessed, possessed creature who throws caution to the winds and heads right into them.

1 ⚬⚬ Mac the Knife

I had always thought we were a happy family. We had everything anybody could reasonably want. Two superb children—one of each kind—a ranch house all brick and glass with no mortgage on it. An acre of trees and hybrid horticulture. A heated swimming pool, fireplaces that worked, a brand-new waffle iron, and season tickets to the Philharmonic. Meals were on time and relatively free of cholesterol. My husband had a wife who got along beautifully with his family, and I had a husband who looked like Gregory Peck and Cary Grant on their better days. *Good Housekeeping* would have given *us* its Seal of Approval and put *his* picture on the cover.

We lived about twenty-five miles from Madison Avenue, where the family breadwinner plowed the wasteland of the television industry, and about twenty-five light-years away from the never-never land of television ratings. Of course, a few minor problems cropped up from time to time. Like on the tenth of every month when the bills came in. Or when the washing machine blew a gasket, or the mailman said he noticed termites in the terrace. Then a low undercurrent gradually reached the proportions of a tidal wave—about the pressures of a competitive society, taxes, home owning, responsibility in general, and commuting in particular.

At these times I was very understanding. I really was. In our house empathy is compulsory. I realized the situation was symptomatic of the Scarsdale or Suburban Syndrome and acknowledged that every man occasionally needs an escape, even from paradise. But I underestimated that need. One day, fifteen years ago, my husband fell in love.

It was a shock when I found out about it. I eavesdropped as he talked with a friend on the phone.

"Wait'll you see her," he was saying, like a man who's just discovered what he's been missing. "She's a honey! A shape as sleek as a racehorse . . . but with plenty in the beam! She makes a fine entrance, with a beautiful flare in her front. She's got an easy, round bottom that's built to take it! You don't have to jockey this one. Man, does she respond. The lightest touch, and she performs. The rougher it gets, the better she likes it! There's no excess weight on this baby. And here's the topper! She won't cost me a barrel of money!"

That last remark really hurt. I took it personally. I could overlook the rest because the object of his affections really wasn't very imposing. Anyone in his right mind could see she'd been around, and had passed through quite a few hands in her day. Moreover, she was definitely undersized. But he thought she was gorgeous.

She was our very first boat.

We first saw her at Mac's Boatyard one summer morning, high off the ground, astraddle two wooden horses. If you've ever been near the seaside, or a lake, or a river, you've seen Mac's. If you've ever looked at watercolors in some quaint little art gallery, you've seen Mac's. A messy, dusty, heaped-up lot with miles of tar-soaked lumber and rusting metal, rotting docks, and an armada of boats in varying stages of decay. It was all very salty and romantic, with sails and masts sticking up in the background so that artists can find those vertical lines they have to paint in their pictures.

Anyway, there was our boat, all twenty-four feet of her, suspended in that marine melting pot like a beached porpoise waiting for a kind fate to put her back into the water. The place was deserted, so we found a rickety ladder and climbed up.

From that minute on, life was never the same.

The future captain walked onto the foredeck and opened wide the door to adventure. I walked below, and opened wide the door to the head. We both had visions. He of wild, wet seas and a thousand distant harbors. I of wild, wet kids and a thousand picnic lunches.

This ocean liner had two V-shaped pads up front, about four feet long. Under them were two thin slats, one of which lifted up to reveal that most essential of bathroom conveniences. On a boat this is called a head, and on this boat, if you didn't duck yours, you soon wouldn't have one. The ceiling was about four feet eight inches high, and I got a vicious picture of my six-foot one-inch captain—decapitated.

The rest of the interior was a triumph of space conservation. In the space of five feet there were a table and two benches, a miniature sink with a kind of Early American hand pump flanked by a two-burner alcohol stove, a cubbyhole designed to function as an icebox, and a rack for two cups and a saucer. You could cook a meal, set the table, wash the dishes, and put a child on the potty without moving an inch. It was so wonderfully compact you couldn't lose one moment making an unnecessary step.

There was just room enough to lose your mind.

Suddenly, like Neptune rising from the dregs, a stranger loomed up over the rail and vaulted to the deck. From under sun-bleached brows, two sincere blue eyes smiled at us. White shirt open at his nut-brown throat, clad in faded dungarees and worn-down sneakers, he held out a horny hand. Salty as the seven seas, he was.

"Welcome aboard," he boomed. "I'm Mac! You folks interested in a boat?" He patted the side. When you buy a car, you kick the tires. When you buy a boat, you pat everything. "This one's a beauty. She is for sure!"

Before we could comment, the aquatic pitchman went on.

"Like new, she is. Belonged to a nice little ol' man only took 'er out on weekends. A Sunday sailor, so to speak. Out the harbor, right back in again. Bet there's not more than twelve hours on her engine." He patted the railing. "Sleeps four, you know," he said to me.

"Four what?" I asked.

His eyes grew tender and understanding.

"Lady, I want you to know this is the very same kinda boat I own. My wife, she wouldn't have nothing else. Get rid of the big boats, she says to me. I want something cozy and compact. Believe me, lady, I've sailed 'em all!"

He patted the wheel and turned to the now and future captain.

"She's a sea kindly boat, and she'll take anything the sea can hand out. Mister, I can see you know a thing or two about boats. You picked the best one in the yard."

Now, Mac the Knife really settled down to business. Abandoning talk for technology, he addressed himself to his peer.

"She's double-planked," he double-talked. "Her ribs are seasoned, and her stringers top grade. Lapstrake made, and batten seamed all through. Her prop thrust is parallel to her plane propulsion, and she's got a planing hull that'll give you eighteen knots in a five-foot quartering sea. She doesn't squat in her wake, and she won't yaw or broach in a breaking inlet!"

He patted the hull.

"Will it float?" I asked.

Nobody bothered to answer, but Marlo—my husband, the captain—finally got a word in.

"How's she powered?" he wanted to know.

"Single screw," said Mac.

"What did the man say?" I demanded.

"One engine," whispered my husband.

Mac took over again.

"Chevy block, six in line, one thirty horse," said he.

He opened a hole in the floor and invited us down with the air of a collector showing off his latest Rembrandt.

"Direct drive, and you'll get three thousand RPM easy. Four to one compression ratio, isolation mounting, prewired terminal blocks, thermostatic temp control."

"How's she do on gas?" queried the other expert.

"Like a lawn mower," purred his new friend.

They stood in rapt admiration of this marine marvel.

"How does the toilet work?" I asked.

"Head!" my husband whispered.

And he patted mine.

We climbed down the ladder and followed Mac into one of the sheds. He swept some greasy rope and a couple of old anchors off two chairs and pulled a sheaf of papers out of his desk.

"Sit down, folks," he invited. "I've got all the information right here. First, let me tell you that this little boat—new—would cost you seven thousand dollars. And, like I said, this boat *is* practically bran' new. A little paint and polish, and it's like you just got 'er outta the showroom!"

He looked at us like a nautical Saint Francis feeding the seagulls.

"How much?" asked Marlo, falling into the baited trap.

"Weel, let me say this," said Mac as though anybody could stop him. "A boat is a kinda personal thing. It's not like buying or selling a piece of furniture. You get attached to a boat. I want to see this one in the right hands. I got a special feelin' for her . . ."

He looked down at his papers, did a quick bit of figuring with his pencil, and came up with:

"For you, because you and that little lady seem to belong together, sixty-one hundred!"

By now we were ashore, and though he may not have had his sea legs yet, on land my provider walks a pretty steady pace.

"Fifty-three," he snapped.

Mac looked at him as though he had just been nailed to the yardarm.

"Look, mister," he pleaded. "I know how important it is to save a buck when you've got a wife and kids hangin' on like barnacles." He looked at me and decided to start over. "What I mean is, there's more than one way to chart a course. We can make it easy with the right kind of financing."

He was talking to the wrong man. Marlo would as soon make a pact with the devil as sign his name to a mortgage. He labors under those quaint, old-fashioned ideas that say what you can't afford, you don't buy. Also, what you buy, you pay for. So he said:

"Fifty-three, right now, in cash. One check."

Mac came about, reefed his sails, dropped anchor, and said, "It's a deal!"

2 ◈ School days, School days...

I would like to halt our personal odyssey for a minute and address myself to any new boat owner. Let me offer him (and especially her) a little general information. Have you ever wondered how many college professors there are in this great land of ours? Well, there are about five hundred and seventy thousand.

Do you know how many boat owners there are? Approximately fifty million! I am not drawing any conclusions from these statistics, other than that we are a large group and we outnumber the intellectuals at least one hundred to one. There are eight thousand and thirty-two types of stock boat models available. From these figures, you may deduce that we are people capable of making decisions, and though we may not be cerebral, we are selective.

There are cabin cruisers, sea skiffs, catamarans, flying bridge cruisers, sport fishermen, houseboats, double-cabin yachts, convertible sedans, Chinese junks, dinghies, racing boats, yawls, ketches, sloops, and prams. There are sailboats, motor boats, motor-sail boats, outboards, inboards, inboard-outboards, gas- and oil-powered boats. They are fashioned of wood, plastic, glass, aluminum, steel, and the stuff of which dreams are made. For these seagoing luxuries, in one year we paid four billion dollars. The dreams themselves came free. It was their upkeep that ran into money.

Generally speaking, boat owners fall into two distinct categories: men and women. This statement is not as simple-minded as it may seem. Next to learning the difference between port and starboard, this is the most basic bit of information a boat owner can acquire. The Power Squadron School makes no mention of this fact. The Power Squadron was originally instituted by, of, and for men. It is a noble institution of learning, manned by seasoned sailors who are dedicated to the proposition that those who go down to the sea in ships need not necessarily go right to the bottom of the sea in those ships. They will tutor the amateur seaman in everything he always needed to know about boats but was too lazy to ask. So, the captain graduated. His first mate was a dropout. She floundered somewhere between the lessons on chart reading and running-time calculations.

The USPS "school" could well expand its curriculum. Along with courses on "Death and Destruction at Sea," "How Not to Break Up in a Breaking Inlet," or "What to Do Until the Coast Guard Comes," they might include a few lessons of equal importance, such as "Must There Be Mildew?" or "Low Cuisine on the High Sea," or "How to Decorate a Cabin So It Won't Look Like Abe Lincoln's."

The Power Squadron course devotes weeks to a discussion of navigational aids and never mentions the greatest navigational aid of all. I am referring, of course, to the little woman down below in the galley. Charts, compasses, radar, and the like are all most helpful in their places. But I challenge any of them to put out a fire on an alcohol stove, calm the baby, make the sandwiches, and serve hot coffee to a screaming crew. All at the same time. And when the captain yells, "All hands on deck!" the Power Squadron should teach him that his wife has only two of them.

These are just a few facts and figures for the uninitiated. Life at sea is, of course, much more than the bare bones of statistics. So now, if you please, I'd like to get back on course.

The A B C's of boating can be learned easily enough—by reading Chapman's *Piloting, Seamanship & Small Boat Handling,* the boatman's bible, or talking to experienced sailors, or attending the Power Squadron School. It is the E's that must be learned through bitter experience. Briefly, they can be listed as Extras, Equipment, and Expenses. The R's follow the E's in a boater's lexicon. They are Repairs, Replacements, and Reimbursements.

We learned these lessons very quickly. After leaving Mac's, we found a boatyard not too far from home. Mac ran our treasure down there and disappeared from our lives. But I am sure he is still busy launching other families on their way to ultimate togetherness.

The next weekend we arrived at the dock loaded with scrubbing brushes, detergents, polish, buckets, and high hopes. We were going to clean her up and try her out. I even had measuring tape for the new curtains and upholstery that the captain didn't know we were going to get.

The owner of the yard, having found us a charming berth between two rows of barnacle-encrusted pilings in back of a gravel barge, came down to inspect his newest tenant.

"We'll haul her tomorrow," he advised us.

"Haul her!" I protested. "We just got her!"

"Lady," the landlord explained, "this boat is four years old. Even a new one has to be hauled, scraped, sanded, painted, varnished, caulked, rerigged, and refitted every season. And we've gotta tune the engine, clean the bilge, correct the compass, and check her for electrolysis."

He turned to Marlo.

"Why don't you folks come into my office and we'll figger out just what you need."

So we gathered up the cleaning tools, rerolled the measuring tape, swallowed the high hopes, and followed him into his executive suite. We sat down and he pulled out a sheaf of papers and a stub of a pencil. I had a funny feeling we'd been here before.

I said, "I don't think I got your name, sir."

"I'm sorry," said he, "my name's MacBain."

"I'll bet everybody calls you Mac," I offered.

"That's right, missus! How'd you know?"

Without waiting for an answer he got down to business.

"We'll just start with the absolute necessities. I figger you need four nylon lines—no, better make it five ..."

His pencil was flashing across the paper.

"An extra propeller—you never know when you'll foul up on a rock—two fire extinguishers, six life jackets, a boarding ladder, a ship-to-shore radio telephone ..."

I stopped him.

"What do we need with a telephone? I hardly know anybody out there in the ocean."

He looked hurt, but patient.

"Lady, how would you get help out there? You can't just holler for the neighbors!"

I conceded he had a point, so he continued.

"You need four fenders, a radio direction finder, the proper charts, a hose."

I felt I could now contribute some saving to the family budget.

"What do I need a hose for?" I asked.

"Saltwater, lady ... you gotta keep ahead of it. We supply

you with fresh water to wash your boat down with, but that's all. You have to hose her down every time you come in. Saltwater corrodes everything!" He was right. It does—including bank accounts and dispositions.

He paused. "You got kids?"

We nodded.

"Then I'd advise you to put a two-man life raft aboard."

I couldn't help it.

"With all those life jackets?" I pleaded. "What for?"

"Because it's a mighty big body of water, that Long Island Sound, missus. You never know how it's gonna act up. And if you wanna really be smart, you'll put in an automatic sniffer."

He anticipated me. "Because your boat burns gas. And there's nothin' like gasoline for explosions. And your nose ain't always reliable when there's loose gas fumes laying around."

I retired from the conversation while he and Marlo went into a huddle. Mr. MacBain made some rapid calculations, added in his share of next year's federal income taxes, and handed over a slip of paper. It itemized service and equipment. It came to a neat one thousand, two hundred and twenty-five dollars.

We staggered out into the sunlight, and Mac escorted us to our car.

"Give my regards to your kids!" he said.

I looked into his sincere blue eyes, nodded, and turned to go.

"And you give ours to Lady Macbeth!" I muttered.

We got into the car.

"Well," I suggested, "I can always get a job as a waitress."

We didn't say another word to each other for some time thereafter. Three glorious days of ecstatic silence.

3 ∞ The Name of the Dame

Normal conversation resumed at a more propitious time. It was rather one-sided, as I was talking to myself. But, sometimes, I find that it is the best way to communicate. Nobody misunderstands you.

It was about two in the morning, and it occurred to me that I was lying next to a man I didn't really know. For ten years I had looked upon him as the ultimate conservative—a practical, plan-ahead, probe-the-future citizen. He had built our home like a fortress. It was fireproof and hurricane proof. He had covered it with waterproof paint, lightning-proof rods, and foolproof insurance. We were prepared for accidents, locusts, depressions, ill health, revolutions, stock-market slumps, old age, and college educations.

And here was this same man, willing—nay eager—to put his wife and children in a cockleshell with only one inch of old lumber between them and a watery grave. Anyone who had to arm himself with impedimenta against explosion, asphyxiation, flash fires, death by drowning, corrosion and collision wasn't pursuing a sport. He was courting disaster!

Suicidal, I thought, that's what it is. A boat is nothing but a glorified do-in-yourself kit. Furthermore, this feckless stranger, who had the temerity to share my bed, had talked me out of a new refrigerator, new draperies, and a subscription to the Fruit of the Month Club—all of which we desperately needed. Was he or was he not the one who went around turning out lights and lecturing the children about the ant and the grasshopper? A man to lean on ... a man to trust ... the salt of the earth.

Well, I thought, there's such a thing as too much salt. So I poked him.

"Skipper, wake up," I said.

"What time is it?"

"Six bells. Your turn to stand watch."

"For God's sake, Mina Bess," he remonstrated. "This is no time to be bitchy."

"That's where you're wrong, Captain. Six bells is the bitching hour."

"Get it over with," he said, sounding martyred.

"There's one thing more we need for the boat."

"There's not another damn thing we need for the boat!"

"This won't cost you anything."

"Impossible!" he snapped.

"We need a name, sir. And I've thought of a good one, sir. Real nautical."

"I'm listening."

"The Star Boarder ... because she's going to eat us out of house and home, sir."

"You're not very funny."

"How about Mal De Mere? That's a French pun ..."

"Puns are an abomination in any language."

"How about 'Encore Aweigh'?" I persisted. "Nautical and theatrical at the same time ..."

"Let's leave show business out of this."

"I see absolutely no reason to get nasty. How about 'The Yankee Schlepper'?"

"Oy vay!"

"'Ahoy Vay' would be better. Why don't you put in two oil engines, and we can call her 'Diesel Do'?"

"Look ... the name has to be personal," he said, sitting bolt upright. "It should have sentiment. Meaning ... Family meaning! Now, good night!"

For a minute silence reigned.

"I've got it!"

"Correction. You're *going* to get it!"

"We'll change our name to Shapiro."

"What the hell are you talking about?" he bellowed.

"Family. We'll change the family name, then we can call our boat 'The Good Ship Hero'."

"That may be the worst ethnic pun in history," he muttered. "Who asked for this?"

"You did! And it won't be the only thing that changed around here!" I groused.

"How about a small but sizable wager to come out of your house money that the change you suggest will cost you a pretty penny?"

"Okay. Fifty bucks," I allowed.

My captain was right, as always. Kind, generous Mac charged us fifty dollars to paint the name *Marlyn I* on the boat. Marlyn comes from the first and last syllables of the names of our children. They are definitely "family."

The most famous poem ever written about the glories of the seafaring life has a line that says, "And all I ask is a tall ship and a star to steer her by." Well, that's a lovely thought. Let's examine it for a minute. Let's say you and that tall ship are out on a dark, foggy night. You can't see the sky, let alone a star. (This has been known to happen.) What then, oh versifier? Or suppose there's not a cloud in the sky. It's clear as a bell. You look for a star and can't get a glimmer of one because it's high noon and stars are very unlikely at that time of day. What now, oh troubadour?

I have absolutely nothing against poets as a rule. It's just that sometimes their reach exceeds their grasp. I would dearly love to match this poet against Mac and let the two of them debate the question of proper boat equipment. My money would be on Mac. Most of it's already there anyway.

Mac called to tell us the *Marlyn* was ready to go. So were we after I packed a few things: coloring books, seasick pills, extra underwear, Thermos bottles, can openers, cookies, sweaters, sunburn lotion, Band-Aids, and the like. We piled into the car and raced down to the boat. There she was! Gleaming white, shining silver sparkling in the sun, the Stars and Stripes fluttering from her stern. It was an emotional moment, like the first time you stand in front of the Lincoln Memorial. The children proudly brought forth a package, which they presented to their father with solemn faces. They stood at attention as he donned their present, a real captain's hat resplendent with gold braid. Daddy had taken on a new dimension. Nelson at Trafalgar couldn't have looked more heroic to his crew. This was family togetherness at its best!

Then, naturally, appeared the fly in the ointment, the flaw in the crystal, the MacBain of my existence. Mac, with the sheaf of papers in his hand. And larceny in his heart.

"Mr. Lewis," he said. "She's shipshape! But we overlooked a few things, so I took the liberty of putting them aboard. You needed an anchor, a searchlight, windshield wipers, and a shoreline. And I'd like your go-ahead on a bow rail and a stern rail. We wouldn't want those kids falling overboard, would we?"

The captain said, "How much?"

Mac smiled.

"Six hundred dollars, but that includes forty-two gallons of gas and a month's dockage."

He handed over the bill.

I was proud of the skipper. He hesitated a full thirty seconds before he answered firmly.

"All right."

We climbed into the boat, and he started the engine. We pulled away from the dock, but Mac had the last word.

"By the way," he shouted, "don't forget your insurance policy! A boat this size shouldn't come to more than four hundred a season!"

I handed the children fishing rods.

"When we get out there," I told them, "you two start fishing. This family's going to keep eating, no matter what!"

4 ∞ Anchors Can Be a Drag

For the next few weeks Long Island Sound was a boatman's Eden. Calm waters, soft breezes, clear skies. We took advantage of the weather to learn, and we learned a lot.

The skipper, never to cut a buoy. I, never to throw garbage to windward. After a few mishaps, I devised a method that proved invaluable. Before letting go with the whole load, you simple toss something small overboard—an eggshell, a crust of bread, a few coffee grounds. If it doesn't come back you're in, and the garbage is out.

We learned, too, that conversation is not essential to communication. The noise of the engine, and the accompanying vibration, made normal speech impossible. Sign language, gestures, and facial expressions sufficed and "eliminated much unnecessary chatter." I use quotation marks because these are my captain's deathless words.

We discovered that the chromium and varnished wood on a boat must be cleaned and polished constantly lest it be eaten away by the salt. This trimming is called bright work.

It should be called stupid work. It's unending and unavailing.

We found out about teak, the product of an East Indian tree highly regarded by ship builders. It's very classy, very durable, and very expensive. Teak is the hardest wood in the world—and the hardest in the world to keep clean. One tiny potato chip will leave a spot as impossible to remove as the stain on Lady Macbeth's little hands.

I personally learned how to prepare hot, tasty meals at sea. You simply cook them at home, wrap them in several layers of insulation, and carry them to the boat.

We experimented with division of labor and instituted a most satisfactory system of specialization. The skipper read the charts, plotted the course, piloted the boat, and called his broker on the ship-to-shore phone. I cast off, tied up, hung the bumpers, removed the bumpers, opened hatches, closed windows, coiled line, leaped from wet decks to wet docks, and dropped and hauled anchor.

Anchoring is a sometime thing and takes a heap of learning. An anchor is a miserable, two-pronged hunk of deadweight metal with a whim of iron. When you want it to hold, the damn thing slithers across the bottom like an eel. When you want it to let go, it sinks itself into the mud with the tenacity of a boa constrictor. Regardlesss of its moods, it will break your back and lacerate your hands. It makes dangerous inroads into the disposition of the pilot, who is trying to maneuver the boat and head into the wind at the same time. When you manage to haul the filthy enemy out of the muck and onto the deck, what it brings with it is too nauseating to describe. So you don't describe it. You just clean it up and try to forget.

One humiliating incident, however, I will never forget. We were lying at anchor in a secluded cove when along came a floating palace that must have belonged to a Greek shipping tycoon. It was about 120 feet long, each of its two dinghies bigger than all of the *Marlyn*. It settled down next to us, and I could see white-jacketed stewards pussyfooting back and forth carrying silver salvers with tall frosted glasses. Everything in sight was monogrammed. Under their starched whites, the crew were undoubtedly branded with the same insignia. A bevy of elegantly dressed characters lounged on the foredeck, waiting for the caviar to chill. The whole thing was ostentatious, vulgar, and thoroughly un-American. I have never been so envious in my life.

Maybe he didn't like the competition, because suddenly my captain gave the order to pull up and get the helm out of there. I tried. And tried. But that oversize fishhook had found the place it liked best in the world. The skipper revved up his engine. He went forward. He went backward. He went sideward. He went berserk, shouting instructions from the bridge. Next door, the jet set had lined up to watch. Just as I felt my back breaking, the anchor came loose.

The leader of the leisure class leaned over his rail. "Hey, buddy, why don't you get a winch?"

I looked at Marlo. He was grinning like a skull and crossbones.

"What's so blessed funny?" I yelled.

"Who needs a winch? I've got a wench!" he chortled in a kind of macabre good humor.

If we had been anywhere else, I would have killed him, walked home, and thrown myself on the mercy of the court.

Never mind what Women's Lib says. The facts are simple. The female of the species differs from the male. And nowhere is this dichotomy of the sexes more apparent than in the business of homemaking. A man's dwelling is a practical structure that affords him shelter, comparative comfort, and a modicum of privacy. His approach is simple, pragmatic, and free of any mystique whatsoever. A woman's home is the one place where she can impose her own brand of order and aesthetic harmony on an otherwise chaotic world.

I am quite sure that when our first ancestor came down from his tree and ushered the little woman into a modern, dry, snug cave, he was chagrined at her reaction. Instead of congratulating him on their move to a better neighborhood, she immediately sent him out to find her a nice saber-toothed tiger skin to drape over the entrance and make the place more homey.

So it was with the captain and me. Operation decor had reached an impasse. What started as a minor skirmish had developed into a serious war. Marlo could see no reason to "make a boat into a boudoir." According to him, the *Marlyn*'s interior was just as it should be: Unadorned and terribly simple. I claimed it was unappealing and simply terrible. The seas of matrimony were getting a bit choppy.

It was raining one afternoon, so we were home. The captain was reading. I was brooding. He was immersed in the latest issue of *Boating* magazine, a fat, glossy periodical dearly beloved by yachtsmen. It was a hundred to one bet that this copy was indistinguishable from all the others that had preceded it down through the years.

There would be a jolly story, written by a happy couple who had converted an old shrimp boat into a three-masted schooner and managed to sail it from Cap Cod to Greece in the middle of the monsoon season. This thriller would be called "To Hellas and Back," or some such awfully clever title. The rest of the publication would be filled with thousands of pictures and descriptions of all the new gadgets no boat owner could afford to do without.

I watched the captain as he read the seductive literature, and I could see him mentally composing a list. Then I broke the spell.

"May I approach the throne, sire?"

"The court will grant no audience till it be St. Swithin's Day," he said without looking up.

"I bring grave tidings of the flagship, excellence!"

"Speak to the prime minister," he said, turning a page. "Go through channels."

"We may never go through channels again, sire. There is mutiny brewing aboard the *Marlyn*!"

"What are you after?" he asked as though he didn't know.

"Not I, sire, the crew. The whole bloody, tired crew! The cook, the mate, the bos'n, the midship mate, the cabin boy, the steward, the deckhands..."

"All right," he said, finally looking up. "I get the point. What do you want?"

"Better living conditions belowdecks, your grace."

"We've been over that. It's unnecessary. It's expensive!"

"Not as expensive as hiring a new crew, sire. On that you can bet your kingdom!"

"O.K.! But remember, this is not Cleopatra's barge you're decorating."

"My compliments, majesty! 'Tis a wise ruler who knows when to give an inch!"

I lost no time. By the weekend the *Marlyn* had new curtains, cushions, dishes, and matching towels. She had new coverings on the floor, the windows, the benches, and the bunks. Drunk with power, I even bolted a basket of artificial flowers onto the table. Then I invited the admiral down for a general inspection. With the air of a strong man who has suffered long and silently, he came in and sat down on the new upholstery. He looked around. He struggled for words.

"It's ... it's ..."

"Adorable?" I prompted.

"Absolutely," he agreed, choking just a little. "By the way, do you think you could prevail upon the cook to make some coffee? And suggest to the steward that he serve it in the new dishes. And while you're at it, give the crew my compliments and ask them if they'd care to join me for a small libation."

So I did.

The captain raised his cup.

"A toast to the crew!" he said.

"And to their victory at sea!" I answered.

And we drank it down.

All of which proves: A little more bounty, a little less mutiny. There was no longer any danger of insurrection aboard the *Marlyn*.

To be absolutely honest, there never had been.

5 ∞ Phone Conversation Piece

Within the boating fraternity there is a subspecies that I call the port sport, a member of the genus dock flock. The port sport has discovered the ultimate status symbol—a boat that never leaves the harbor. It is beautifully maintained and looks new. It should. Its owner never gets it wet. His boat is as dry as the martinis served every day to the dock flock.

And they have all discovered the ultimate cocktail lounge, the afterdeck of a boat. Nothing compares with it. The lapping of water against the sides provides the perfect background for the lapping of liquor over the tongue. The flock can get thoroughly tanned and tanked at the same time.

The port sport doesn't know his aft from his elbow, which he is constantly bending. The only equipment he uses are his swizzle sticks, his ice bucket, and his radio-telephone.

The United States government has issued directives concerning the use of such phones. They say that conversation should be limited to matters of urgent ship's business so that distress signals, calls for help, and emergency measures can receive immediate attention. The dock flock has its own definition of "urgent ship's business."

For instance, there was the day we set forth to rendezvous with an important star of stage, screen, and radio, whom my captain was wooing for an important new television show. Preparations for this historic meeting had taken a bit of doing, as this particular luminary lived by his own commandments and demanded a similar subscription from everybody around him. He was, to put it simply, a stickler.

Everything had to be perfect. He expected a salad fork beside his salads. He piled magazines according to publication dates and made sure all their corners were in alignment. He had his towels folded so that the monograms were always in the center. But above all, this man made of punctuality a virtue next to godliness.

Now, although I had always been of the school that contends there are no stars except in heaven, I had once more been persuaded that the realities of life dictate otherwise. Since six o'clock that sunny morning, I had been coping with the logistics of the situation. The wine was on ice, the gourmet luncheon in its baskets, the correct cutlery aboard, the teak washed and the chromium polished, the cushions plumped, the lines coiled with jeweler's precision, and the captain in starched whites on the bridge. Our rendezvous with the star of stage, screen, radio, and, we hoped, television, was to be across the bay, on a dock, at exactly one o'clock. By eleven the skies were blue and the sun was hot. The day was perfect. Except for an incongruous wind that sprang up from nowhere like a banshee and turned the Sound into a boiling caldron. There was no fighting it.

The captain, who is in his own way a philospher, said, "To hell with it."

Turning his ship toward the shelter of the nearest shoreline, he gave orders.

"Get him on the phone. Tell him what's happened. Thank God that fussy bastard's still at home. If he was waiting at the dock and we didn't show up, we'd blow the whole deal."

I knew it was no use before I had even picked up the phone. This was high noon on Sunday, the time we used to tune in to what we called "The Long Island Sound Off" or the "Alcoholics Unanimous Hour." This was the time the dock flock regularly conducted their business, the time you could be adrift or afire and never find a channel on your ship-to-shore phone through which to broadcast your cry for help as you stood on the burning deck.

As I switched on the phone, I heard them.:

Boat A: Calling the *Lucky Bubble*. Calling the *Lucky Bubble*. This is the *Shirley's Diamond*. Come in, *Lucky Bubble*.
Boat B: This is the *Shirley's Diamond*. Come in, *Lucky Bubble*. Over.
Boat A: How do you read me, *Shirley's Diamond?* Over.
Boat B: Loud and clear, Sol! How're you feeling after last night? Over.
Boat A: Feeling absolutely no champain, Irv. Ha! Ha!. Over.
Boat B: Mazeltov! How's Francine? Over to you.
Boat A: Still in bed. She's got an icebag on her head as big as the bags under her eyes. How's Shirley? Over to you.
Boat B: Let's not talk about any more bags, pal. Over.
Boat A: What're your plans, fella? Over.
Boat B: Whatdaya say we rendezvous about three? Over.
Boat A: Roger! What's your position? Over.
Boat B: We're still at the dock. Where are you? Over.
Boat A: About thirty feet abaft your starboard beam, Sol! Over.

Boat B: Come on, Irv. Don't give me that captain's talk. Where the hell are ya? Over.
Boat A: Two docks to the right of you, schmuck! Over.
Boat B: Whyn't you say so! That makes it easy. See you at three. Over to you.
Boat A: Roger! I'll bring the gin cards. You get out the gin. Over.
Boat B: Great. This is the *Lucky Bubble* signing off to the *Shirley's Diamond.* Over and out.

After Sol and Irv, we listened to Barry and Harry, Gary and Larry, Damon and Pythias. On Sunday afternoon they are never over and never out.

Needless to say, the captain blew his top because he knew we had blown the deal. The star stickler never forgave us and went on to shine on a rival network where, presumably, nobody ever kept him waiting.

It should be apparent by now that not everything that menaces a boatman is confronted at sea. There are things onshore that present equal hazards—like the dock flock. On the other hand, in their constant state of euphoria, it is just as well that this group of marinated mariners never leave their homeport. Without question, the whole flotilla would wind up like its bonded scotch—straight on the rocks!

6 ∞ Special Delivery

Long before "guilt by association" became a term of opprobrium, "birds of a feather flock together" was an honored bit of simple folk wisdom. Experience has prejudiced me toward the latter view.

I have noticed that neurotics love to suffer with other neurotics. Crackpots consort with fellow crackpots. And boat owners enrich their lives by seeking out other boat owners. How else can I explain my close friendship with Donna Brooks?

To begin with, she was a full six feet from stem to stern, and before the two of us could see eye to eye, or talk heart to heart, Donna had to sit down. She was working her way through marriage number four, while I was still walking ten paces behind the same man. Moreover, Donna was irrevocably committed to blood-rare meat, Ingmar Bergman movies, Freudian analysis, and the agrarian reform program of the Soviet Union.

She had raised packs of slavering Great Danes, acres of

writhing, obscene tropical orchids, thousands of dollars for Russian War Relief, and hell with four husbands. She had never found the time to raise any children.

Normally, we would have rejected Donna on the grounds that she was a frivolous, spoiled, overprivileged, underworked parasite, and a political cretin to boot. But she was a skilled and dedicated boatwoman, worth her not inconsiderable weight in gold doubloons to any ship she sailed on. So we became dear friends.

Donna's latest venture into matrimony had taken her to live in Florida. Thus it was that one midwinter weekend, when the captain and I found ourselves in Fort Lauderdale, he suggested I call her.

"Why?" I asked.

"Because we haven't seen her for almost a year, and it would be the nice thing to do."

I studied the back of his head. He was looking out of the window at the marina below, where boats of all sizes were floating like a covey of sleek white ducks.

"I wonder if this is where she keeps it," he murmured.

"Where who keeps what?" I asked.

"Where Donna keeps her boat."

"I'll call her," I said. "Because it's the nice thing to do."

A few minutes later I heard her booming, slightly gritty voice on the phone.

"Greetings, comrade," I said.

"Hello, Angel! Where are you?"

"Right here in sunny Florida."

"Marvelous!" she cried.

"What's new, Donna?"

"So much I don't know where to begin. For one thing, I have a marvelous new husband."

"I know. I was at the wedding."

"You were at my third wedding."

"I was at *all* your weddings. What's this one's name, again?"

"Biff. He's a darling. And I have a new pair of Great Danes that are bound to win 'best of breed' in the next show."

"What are their names?" I took the bait.

"Get Off The Couch and You Too. And I have a simply super new boat. Specially built with twelve inches extra headroom. Biff is six five, and he was always cracking his skull against something."

"What's the boat's name?"

"*Tovarich.*"

"That figures. Which leads me to the next question. What's new on the community action front?"

"Very little, pet," she said with a sigh. "I had planned a really gorgeous party for Jane Fonda when she was down here organizing the southern state colleges, but I just haven't been up to it."

"Aren't you well, Donna?"

"Oh, I'm fine. I'll tell you about it when I see you."

"When'll that be?" I wanted to know.

"How about tomorrow around eight at the *Tovarich?* We'll head for the Keys."

"I'll see if I can persuade the skipper. Where's she docked?"

"At the Sunshine Marina. You won't have any trouble finding her."

"I know. She'll be the only boat there flying the Hammer and Sickle."

I hung up and turned to the captain. "I'm really worried about Donna. She hasn't done one solitary thing lately for the Underdeveloped Nations Yearning To Be Free From the Yoke of Western Imperialism."

A look of genuine concern crossed his face. "I hope the boat's in good shape," he said.

The next morning, as he stood in front of the *Tovarich*

scrutinizing her forty-eight feet, the skipper displayed little enthusiasm.

"She's top-heavy," he admonished me. "She's big, but out of proportion."

Just then I glanced up, and I saw Donna come through the hatch onto the deck. For one frozen moment I looked at her, then I clutched the skipper's arm. "Say it again, Sam," I told him. "Then look up slowly."

"She's big," he repeated, "and out of proportion ... Oh, my God!"

Donna was in full view. And she was pregnant! Pregnant as no other woman before. Like an avant-garde sculptor's dream of the ultimate fertility goddess. Swollen, monolithic, mind-boggling.

I could only gasp. "How come?"

Donna simpered. "The usual way."

"I mean *why*? That's what I mean! Why?"

She drew herself up as best she could. "Because I'm forty-two years old, and it's now or never. I got to thinking, to whom am I going to leave all that money? It's such a lot of money, you know. And I will not have my ex-husbands quarreling over my grave. I need an heir."

"You need your head examined," I snapped. "Why didn't you just leave it to the Chicago Seven? Think of all the lovely bombs they could have bought! Or the American Civil Liberties Union."

"They're already in my will." She shrugged. "What's done is done. Let's decide where we want to go today."

"I vote for the nearest maternity ward," said Marlo.

"Don't be silly," said the future mother of Hercules. "I'm only in my eighth month. Let's head for Key Largo."

So while she charted the course, and Marlo took the wheel, I went below to inspect the living quarters. They were magnificent. Spacious and airy and expensive—and absolutely unbearable. Belowdecks the *Tovarich* pitched and rolled with relentless intensity. I staggered up to the pilothouse and confronted the captain. "What's the matter with this goddamned boat?" I asked him. "No living thing could survive down there."

"It's the goddamned superstructure." He was very patient. "I told you she was top-heavy."

"And I'm telling you, if we starve to death I will not set foot in that galley again."

"Go lie down on the foredeck. You'll feel better up there," he suggested.

That was good advice. For two blissful hours I slept, until something woke me. That something was the good old *Tovarich*, lurching and wallowing in stomach-curdling gyrations. We were surrounded by choppy seas, in the middle of nowhere. Clinging to the rail, I made my way aft. Donna was holding on to the pilot's seat.

"Where is he?" I asked.

"In the engine room, I hope." She clapped a hand to her mouth and lurched to the side. By now I knew that the bowels of the ship could be no worse than her decks, so I went below. My captain was on a ladder, poking into four feet of brine.

"This goddamned boat is top-heavy," I told him. "Also, what are you doing and why have the engines stopped?"

"I am trying to find where the plug has blown out of the engine block so I can stop it up and prevent the boat from filling up with water. And I've stopped the engines because each revolution of the props drives more of the sea into the bilges, so get the hell up there and tell Donna to call the Coast Guard."

That last business about calling for help I understood, so I went back to Donna. She had left the rail and was now lying in a pool of liquid, clutching her belly and moaning low. I went back to the engine room. I was very calm.

"Donna cannot call the Coast Guard, or anybody else. Except maybe Almighty God. She has blown her own plug, and there is no way to put it back."

"What are you talking about?"

"Donna's water broke!" I was no longer calm. In truth, I was screaming. "The baby's coming! You call the Coast Guard. I'm going to boil some water!"

"What are you going to do with it after you boil it?"

"How do I know? I just know that's what they do in the movies. And after that somebody comes to help and everything's all right."

I propped a pillow under Donna's head, and the skipper started pressing buttons on the phone. "Coast Guard, calling the Coast Guard. This is the *Tovarich*. Come in. Come in. Over. May Day May Day Over. Where in the bloody hell is the Coast Guard? Where is Donna's husband? That dumb son of a bitch. His wife is having a baby, and his boat is sinking."

"I'll tell you where he is," I yelled. "He's where every sensible man in Florida is today! He's at the Super Bowl watching the Miami Dolphins play whoever it is. And I bet that's where the Coast Guard is. Over and out to you!"

The ship-to-shore phone suddenly crackled to life. "This is the Coast Guard. We read you, *Tovarich*. Come in. Over."

"*Tovarich* to Coast Guard," said my Marlo in the calm voice he uses to explain a drop in the ratings. "We have an emergency. Engine inoperable, shipping water, request a tow, also a doctor. There is a woman aboard having a baby. Over."

"Holy Mother!" barked the Coast Guard. "Do you know what day this is, *Tovarich*? Over."

"It's May Day here, buddy. May Day. Over."

"It's also Super Bowl Day in Miami, pal. Every doctor in town is at the game. This is gonna take a little time. State your position. Over."

So the captain stated his position, which was up the creek

a little behind the eight ball and approximately between the devil and the deep blue sea. Donna stopped groaning long enough to state her position, which as always, was somewhat left of center.

"In a progressive society," she informed us, "doctors would be directly responsible to the state, not wasting their time watching mercenaries maim each other in commercial arenas while citizens perished by the wayside."

"In a progressive society," snarled the captain, "you would be declared an enemy of the state for owning a three hundred thousand dollar boat like this friggin' tub in the first place."

We wedged ourselves against Donna to keep her from rolling around too violently and settled down to wait. After an eternity, the blessed Coast Guard came back on the air.

"*Tovarich*, this is the Coast Guard. You're in luck. We found a doctor who doesn't like football. He doesn't like boats either, but we got him. Over."

"You are a great group, Coast Guard. How long? Over."

"About forty-five minutes. Hold on, pal. Over and out."

I will always remember the next sixty minutes as life's darkest hour. Donna's pains were zeroing in every few minutes by the time the Coast Guard cutter pulled up alongside. The young seaman who scrambled up the boarding ladder cast a professional eye on the whole scene, shifted a wad of chewing gum from one suntanned cheek to the other and addressed us. "This goddamned boat is top-heavy," he said.

"By cracky, I never noticed," said the captain, putting out his hand. "Welcome aboard, mister."

Our rescuer stared down at Donna. "She don't look so good either," he decided.

"That's one thing we have noticed," I told him. "Where's the doctor?"

"He'll be up in a minute, lady. But I gotta warn you. He looks worse than she does."

The Coast Guard was right on target again. The plump, bespectacled little man who came struggling up the side looked like a terminal case of acute nausea.

"That the patient?" he croaked, peering at Donna through salt-smeared glasses. "She can't be moved into the other boat?"

"Not without a derrick, she can't," Marlo agreed. "What'll we do?"

"Get her into a bunk," the doctor ordered.

Three stalwart sailors from the cutter's crew hauled Donna down to the main stateroom and lowered her onto the bed.

"Now get me into the other bunk," said the doctor. "Because if I try to hold my head up one more minute, I'll heave the final lining out of my intestines and die." He lay down carefully and closed his eyes. "I'll probably die anyway. Get me the captain."

"Do you want a burial at sea?" I asked, leaning over him.

"Not yet. Later. After I've instructed the captain."

And that's how Donna's baby entered the world. All ten pounds four ounces of him. He arrived while the Coast Guard towed us across choppy seas ... while I boiled water ... while the doctor issued instructions from his bed of pain ... while the captain hurled himself into the breech and followed orders.

At the very end—when he held up that lusty, squirming infant and smacked him across his keel—the captain looked to me like a combination of Marcus Welby, Wyatt Earp, and Sir Galahad all put together larger than life, a hero worthy of another great and glorious saga of the sea.

7 ◈ Weigh Off Broadway

We were a different breed of sailors. We sailed.

To Marlo seawater was more heady than wine, and sea air completely intoxicating. Harbor hovering was not his idea of the good life, and he felt it was time for a real, overnight trip. We considered going to Cape Cod, Martha's Vineyard, or Lake Champlain.

We settled for Stratford, Connecticut. This lovely little town offered the summer visitor a Shakespeare festival, performed in a wonderful replica of the old Globe Theatre. We had never been there because it was a full forty-five minutes from home by car. By boat it was only four running hours. The town is nestled on the banks of the Connecticut River, where a boatman can dock in a charming harbor and walk a short distance to the theater.

We started out one Friday afternoon, prepared for our first weekend afloat. On the way I thought to ask the captain what play we were going to see.

"*The Tempest*," he told me.

"Oh," I commented.

"What's the matter? I thought you loved it."

He seemed a bit put out.

"Oh, I do," I assured him. "But do you think it augers well for a first sea voyage?"

He stopped dead in his tracks.

"Whence comes this sudden medieval turn of mind?" he demanded. "Look at this weather!"

And it was beautiful. Not a cloud in the sky, and the water so still it was glassy. I rubbed suntan oil over myself and stretched out on the foredeck. The boat churned along on a mirror-smooth sea and made her own little breeze as she traveled.

This was boating!

At about five o'clock we headed into the mouth of the river and pulled into the dock. I hung the bumpers and tied her up. It was quaint, utterly charming, picturesque, and hot as the hinges of a blast furnace. Whatever breeze we had stirred up out in the open water had disappeared in the harbor. The sky was brassy, the air was dead, and I was suddenly one overall mass of itching discomfort. The combination of heat, salt, oil, and sun had produced a state bordering on dementia. All I could think of was a shower—a long, cold shower followed by total immersion in powder and cologne.

The captain had gone into the cabin and managed to clean himself up with the help of the little hand pump that peeped shyly out of our tiny sink. A timid and reticent instrument at best, it emitted a reluctant trickle of water when attacked by a strong and implacable hand. The captain had the proper touch. He came forth, sleek as a seal, and departed to get the tickets for the evening's performance.

I made a dash below and started to pump. There wasn't a drop of water left in that toy contraption. It was like seeing an oasis after a long journey across the Sahara and having it turn into a mirage just as you reached a palm tree.

There is no spur to inspiration like desperation. I grabbed a blanket and some towels and went out on the deck. From the canvas top that shaded the pilot's wheel, I draped the blanket and the towels. They didn't reach all the way to the deck, but they covered the strategic areas. Then I went out on the dock, connected the hose, and dragged it back into the boat. I poked the nozzle through the blanket at the top, threw off my clothes, grabbed a can of shaving soap, and turned on the spray.

Heaven!

No raja's ransom, no treasure of the Incas could have paid for that moment.

It must have been ten blissful minutes later that I heard a bellow like an outraged whale. I looked through the gap at the bottom of my curtain and saw a pair of feet ankle-deep in soap suds.

"What in the name of Allah are you doing?" came the voice of authority.

"What does it look like?" I replied. "I'm swabbing the deck!"

Ask a ridiculous question and that's the kind of answer you get.

He stuck his head in.

"They're lined up ten deep on the docks!" he hissed. "You've provided a better spectacle than any play this town can offer! Two scalpers have made a fortune selling front-row standing room."

The injustice of it all was just too much for me.

"Well!" I screamed, "you go tell those nosy dockhundts that a man's boat is his forecastle!"

And I made a dignified but clean withdrawal into my stateroom.

The rest of the evening was lovely, from supper to Shakespeare. By about eleven o'clock *The Tempest* was over.

Onstage, that is. Outside it had only begun. When we walked out of the theater, we walked into a deluge. We stood under the marquee wondering whether to wait a little or make a run for it.

The answer came to me suddenly.

"We've got to go. Now!"

"Why?"

"Because of the hatch."

"What about the hatch?"

"I forgot to close it."

"How . . . how did you manage to forget a thing like that!"

"It was easy. I just said over and over 'forget to close it,' 'forget to close it.' And I remembered to forget! I'm Mina Bess, the memory expert. Knows nothing, remembers everything."

And we started to run. I had a picture of that poor little boat, completely underwater. But she wasn't. She was out of the water, suspended at a sixty-degree list to her port.

"My God," said the captain. "This isn't a floating dock! I forgot to allow for the tide!"

Right then and there, I exercised superhuman forebearance. I did not ask a searching question. With saintly patience, I suggested that what goes down must come up, and that eventually—if the lines didn't snap or the dock collapse—when the tide came up, the *Marlyn* would settle down. The idea met with no enthusiasm. Nothing would do but to put the situation right. Right then.

Have you ever tried to loosen taut, wet ropes with five tons straining against them? While the wind blows? And the rains pelt down? At midnight? If you have to, forget it! Even if you don't have to, forget it.

When we finally floundered aboard, the real fun began. Everything that wasn't nailed down was a scrambled mess.

The bunks were a sodden mass of sheets and blankets. So we mopped and we sopped and we stowed and we stewed. At 2:00 A.M. we finally lay down. I was so tired I could have fallen asleep on a bed of nails. It would have been a luxury compared to that bunk.

Putting it mildly, it was damp, dank, and sticky. The skipper took up his side, half of mine, and was slowly edging me out of the two feet I had left. The boat rocked and creaked and rolled in a relentless frenzy all night long. We couldn't open the windows because of the rain, and it was hot and airless and choking. A night to remember. The final indignity came with one lone mosquito that was furious at being trapped in this particular swamp and was out for revenge.

I began to think of our bedroom at home. The air conditioner purring away. The king-size bed with the sweet, smooth, satin sheets. The oversize bathroom with its beautiful twentieth century plumbing. Which led me to a frightening thought. What would happen if someone wanted to use that ridiculous thing crouching under the bunks?

This way lay madness! I had to pursue a different line of thought or run howling into the night. So I began to compose some poems. Some people count sheep, some people drink hot milk, some people take pills. But I play with words. This results in more therapy than poetry, but it worked and I lived to see the dawn, which came not one minute too soon. If you care to read what came out of my sleepless agony, you will find it at the end of this chapter.

After one look into the icebox, we went ashore for breakfast. The man at the counter looked cheerful and friendly. Obviously he had spent the night at home in bed.

So I asked him, "How fare the winds for Troy?"

It was a pardonable query when you consider I had spent my night with the muse. But he thought I was talking to myself.

"She means what's the weather report?" said Marlo.

"Rough," he told us. "Seems there's a hurricane down in Florida, and it's gonna raise all hell with the whole New England Coast. Seas are going to chop up 'fore the day's over."

We took one look at each other and started to run. We got back to the boat, revved up, cast off, and started down that river without a backward glance. At the mouth of the river I found out what a breaking inlet is. It's a place that will let you in but won't let you out. The water swirls and heaves where the open sea begins. The currents fight each other and you're caught in the middle of an undeclared war. It's like being a cork in a whirlpool. You can't go back, and you don't want to go on.

William Shakespeare may have written *The Tempest*, but we lived it. After ten minutes of eternity, thanks to a steady, foolhardy hand at the wheel, we got through it. I found myself patting the boat and murmuring, "Good girl, good girl!"

But the good girl still had her work cut out for her. The sea was an infinity of swollen, oily, waves. The *Marlyn* slid up one, then pitched down into the trough. But the skipper was a man of fortitude. He remembered from his surfing experience that if you can get on the crest of a wave, it will carry you along with it. We had a following sea, so he found one crest after another and fought to stay on them. That's how we got home.

When we turned into our harbor I went up to the bow, all ready to jump down and kiss the dock. I was standing there with the line in my hand and a song in my heart when I heard the captain yell:

"Fend her off!"

The crazy winds and currents were driving us right into a piling. The order from the bridge had come in the nick of time. The only trouble was, we didn't have a boat hook. That was one thing Mac the Knife No. 2 had overlooked!

"Fend her off!" I heard again.
"With what?" I yelled back.
"Who cares!" the captain shouted.
So I stuck my legs out just as we careened by that transplanted telephone pole. We slid into our berth with a hair's breadth to spare, and I leaped down onto the dock.
"Any damage?" yelled the captain.
"Only a couple of scratches," I assured him.
"Which side? Port or starboard?"
I looked at my shins.
"Both," I answered.
"How deep are they?" came the anxious question.
"Not very. They're just bleeding moderately."
"Oh," he said with palpable relief. "For a minute you had me worried!"
You have to understand his viewpoint. After all, I had two legs. He had only one boat. My other vital statistics didn't stack up well either, compared with the *Marlyn*.

	Marlyn	*Me*
Length Over-All	26 feet	5 feet 1 inch
Gross Weight	3 tons	105 pounds
Beam	10 feet	A lot less
Power	125 horsepower	1/2 pony power

A Married Man's Soliloquy at the Boat Show

To buy or not to buy: that is the question
Whether 'tis nobler in the end to suffer
The cost and burdens of outrageous upkeep
Or to take stand against a sea of debits
And by refusing, end them. To buy: to sell
Once more; and buy to sell to say we end
The heartache, and the thousand natural bills
A boat is heir to. 'Tis a consummation
Devoutly to be wished. To buy, to own;
To own? Perchance to owe! Aye there's the rub;
Thus marriage does make cowards of us all,
And thus the native flush of inspiration
Is sicklied o'er with thought of hearth and home
And enterprises of great joy and import
In duty's name must craven slink away
And man is drowned in husbandry.

How to Handle a Husband at Sea

Pipe him aboard when you set sail
Laugh with joy when it blows a gale
Never admit to mal de mer
Encourage the wind to ruin your hair
Babble about the sea's mystique
Hose the deck and scrub the teak
Batten hatches and stow the gear
Heat the coffee and ice the beer
Clean the bilges and scrape the brine
Haul the anchor and coil the line
Hang each fender, reef the sail
Lower the tender, walk the rail
Hop to it, lass, when you're aboard
And maybe as a small reward
When you've polished all the chrome
He'll let you spend next weekend home!

Ballad of the Regrettable Regatta

'Twas on the beach I saw the maid
    A lonely vigil keeping
And I was truly much afraid
    To hear such sorry weeping.

"Pray tell," I said, "What makes you cry
    And moan so grievously?"
She wiped a tear from out her eye
    And answered thus to me.

"My sweetheart was a sailor boy
    Proud owner of a sloop
And she was his true pride and joy
    The fastest of her group!

"There was to be a final race
    And my love did promise me
That if I helped him win first place
    His own true bride I'd be!

"I begged him for a chance to show
    How skillful I could be
My sailor gladly went below
    And left the helm to me.

"We ran before the wind, my friend
    We flew before the tide
Our goal was near and at the end
    I'd be the captain's bride!

"Yet though I held fast to the wheel
    Oh, never-ending grief
I felt a scraping 'neath the keel
    I'd run her on a reef!

CONFESSIONS OF A BOAT LOVER'S WIFE

"I knew that though he'd lost the prize
    I'd lost the best in life
Full fathom five my hope now lies
    To be the captain's wife!"

"Oh, how you must regret," I cried
    "The day you went to sea!"
She shook her head as she replied
    And answered thus to me

"Though I have learned through grievous cost
    Pride goeth 'fore a fall
'Tis better to have luffed and lost
    Than never to have luffed at all!"

My Ship

My ship has decks of the finest teak
Bronze fittings in her hold
And if she ever springs a leak
We'll patch her up with gold!

Our boat is like a work of art
She's sweet as wine and homey
And if she starts to come apart
We'll calk her seams with money!

My ship's equipped with the latest gear
She lacks no single thing
But if she did, our path is clear
We'd hock my wedding ring!

Her faithful engines turn and toil
We speed with style and dash
We give them neither gas nor oil
The fuel they burn is cash!

My craft is rigged from aft to fore
With goodies we have bought 'er
If we indulge her one time more
We'll live on bread and water!

We toast our ship—Our lady fair
Salud - Santé - L'chaim!
And though I'd like some clothes to wear
There's nothing left to buy 'em!

8 ∞ The Captain Flips

That night I fought against sleep. Not that I wasn't dead tired. But everything was so comfortable and so lovely, I didn't want to miss a minute of it.

Evidently Lord Nelson wasn't asleep either, because his muffled voice spoke from under the pillow where he snored softly any night he didn't want to hear what I said.

"You've got to admit, it was an experience!" He was enthusiastic.

"So's an appendectomy," I retorted.

"What did you say?"

"I said this bed feels like a deck to me."

"That'll pass. You're still rocking."

"Sideways?"

"You know, I've decided I don't like a flat bottom."

"I've always hoped you felt that way."

"And a single screw is not enough."

"I will not argue the point," I conceded.

"I've decided to sell her."

I lay in absolute, unbelieving silence.

"I said, I have decided to sell the boat," he said again.

"Funny thing, for a moment I thought you said you've decided to sell the boat."

"I did."

"After all the money we spent! After all the time we spent! After all the energy we spent! I thought you loved her!"

"She's inadequate. I'm just being practical."

"Mon Capitaine, je vous adore!"

"What does your first-year French have to do with selling the boat?" he asked.

"It takes a big man to admit he's made a mistake. To profit by experience. To take his losses and go on to bigger and better ventures."

"Naturally. That's how I know exactly what to look for in our next boat."

"I must see my otolaryngologist tomorrow. Unless I didn't hear you say 'our next boat.' "

"You've got a pair of great ears. Among other things. We'll have a fabulous time next summer," he prophesied.

"The vibrations have affected my hearing! I could swear you said we'd go abroad next summer. What you said was we'll go aboard next summer. Right?"

"Europe will be there a long time."

"Ah, well. They say Spain is hot, and Rome is dirty. Trips that pass in the night. . .

"I knew you'd understand. By the way, how about a date some night?"

"We'll have to wait until my husband's away at sea."

"Too bad. I know that no-goodnick. He'll never set sail without you."

The winter passed quickly. It always does if you go away for a while. Some of our friends went east to the beaches of the Mediterranean. Some went west to the tennis courts of

Palm Springs. Others went north to the ski slopes of Vermont. We went south to a boatyard in New Jersey.

As it was explained to me, there is a small town down there, which we will call Chowder Head. For generations the best Jersey sea skiff in the world has been made there. A Jersey Chowder Head is a boatman's boat—a seaworthy, handmade, utterly rugged sport fisherman designed to weather all the storms and rough weather the Jersey coast can hand out.

For the uninitiated, a sport fisherman is a sturdy open cockpit boat with a flying bridge from which the pilot can see how to maneuver around the fishing lines that trail behind. A small trunk cabin that provides small comfort but adequate shelter from blistering sun, pelting rain, or murderous wind, a large aftdeck equipped with swivel chairs from which the sport can cavort with rod and reel, and, if he's lucky, mess up with the thrashing carcass of some dying great white whale. Ernest Hemingway, for instance, when he was not trudging through the bush on safari, or shouting olé at the bullring, could be found on the aftdeck of a sport fisherman.

So every Saturday, through rain, and snow, and sleet and fog, we'd take the scenic route. Through the tunnel and onto the turnpike, one hundred miles each way, past oil refineries, fertilizer factories, power plants, and chemical smelters. After a while, I could tell just where we were without opening my eyes. The aromas that filled the air were sure signposts of each industrial area we entered.

Our first sight of the little factory that handcrafted one hundred Chowder Heads a year was encouraging. It was neat and organized and smelled so aromatically of seasoned wood and fresh varnish that you knew you were in the presence of real old-fashioned American artisanship. You knew it absolutely when you were in the presence of the head man, whose great grandfather, old Abel MacDour, had founded the business. He spoke of his boats the way a nineteenth-century ship builder must have referred to a Gloucester-built schooner out of Maine. In fact, the present MacDour *was* a nineteenth-century boat builder. Behind his rolltop desk he kept a hawk eye on every mote of sawdust that fell.

"Got no use for these slick, mass-produced commercial barrel staves they call boats nowadays," he said to Marlo. "No pride in 'em . . . Take a look around. You could eat off this floor!"

Marlo was impressed, but I was only mildly thrilled. I was brought up to eat at a table, except on picnics. For me, these visits were no picnic.

MacDour managed to overlook my presence as though I had never been born. Apparently there were two things in this world he resented, besides the arrival of the twentieth century. One was any suggestion that his boats could be improved in any way. The other was women. Both were superfluous, troublesome, and frivolous. I'm sure that when MacDour finally sails into that last big harbor in the sky and faces the Great Shipwright, he will refuse heaven itself if any females are seen cluttering up the celestial seas.

In the meantime he spoke only to Marlo, leaving me to my own devices.

The first few weeks I passed the time by sending postcards to my friends. I bought them at the local emporium, which carried a fascinating stock of rope splicers, hawsers, fishing tackle, and foul-weather gear. The cards had wonderful scenes of the Chowder Head post office, high school, and poultry feed warehouse, built by the WPA in 1936. I must have made the town famous all over the world. For instance, I sent one to Italy:

Dear Millie,
Come sta a Portofino? Had a lovely time today at a quaint little bistro called Howard Johnson. The natives

are not too friendly. Hope you can join us on the new yacht this summer.

Or

Dear Ellie,

Hope you have enough snow on the slopes over there in St. Moritz. Down here we are lucky. The drifts are five feet high and getting higher!

Or

Dear Roberta,

Read your *Lucia* was a triumph in Mexico City. Sorry we can't meet you in Acapulco, but we're spending the season at this picturesque little seaside town. Give up the high C's for the high seas with us this summer! Till then.

After a while the store ran out of postcards, and I ran out of friends. So I decided to make a needlepoint sampler for the boat. The day I started working on it, MacDour nearly choked. I explained that this handicraft, too, was in the best tradition of old American artisanship.

Marlo was apologetic. "She's making it for the boat," he explained, thinking this would mollify the old goat.

It had the opposite effect. Mac uttered the final undeleted expletive.

"Women!" he barked, and henceforth avoided me like Jonah.

As for the boat, she was very much like the old one. Bigger, of course. A full thirty feet. There were two engines this time, an electric pump for the water pressure. And glory in the highest, a stand-up head! This concession to the present era consisted of a closet with a door that would close, a minuscule washbasin, and a little medicine chest with a mirror.

This was a luxury yacht.

She also cost twice as much. But she was a Chowder Head, and worth every penny.

Our new flagship also had a special navy top. This means that instead of a hard roof over the pilot's wheel on the deck, a canvas roof was constructed that could be rolled back so the captain could stand in the sun. It represented a great departure for MacDour. He didn't approve of it. He didn't believe in it. He had never made one. But such was their friendship by now that he agreed to try it for Marlo. This colossal feat of retooling and redrafting took weeks of persuasion. The fact that Detroit turned out millions of convertibles every year impressed him not at all. He reacted the way his great grandfather had when someone suggested converting from sail to steam.

By the end of the winter we had done three thousand miles to New Jersey and back. The *Marlyn II* had been completed. The captain had two engines. My sampler was ready to be framed. And who was I to say that a depleted bank balance wasn't worth these blessings?

April 12 was delivery day, and no visit from the stork was ever awaited with more impatience. MacDour was as good as his word. On the night of the twelfth we were informed that our boat was waiting for us at the home yard. The robins were back, the tulips were up, the voice of the turtle was heard in the land. And that night it snowed for eight hours.

The next morning we dug ourselves out, put chains on the car, and skidded our way to the boatyard. There was the *Marlyn II* parked next to the big storage shed. With about five tons of wet snow on her aftdeck. The accumulated mass had slid off the roof of the building, and with unerring accuracy had landed right in the middle of MacDour's masterpiece! The *Marlyn* had literally blown her navy top. What was left was a tangled heap of torn canvas, twisted metal and slush.

I struggled for words.

"Well, at least we know the boating season has really arrived!"

The captain looked at me the way Ahab must have looked at Moby Dick.

"How do you figure that one?" he snarled.

"Because, blizzard or no blizzard, the sure signs are here. A minor catastrophe, followed by a major expenditure!"

Something about the situation suggested to me that it would not be propitious to unveil my sampler at that moment. I had hopefully brought it along, and it truly was beautiful. The design had been worked in the shape of a shield. There was a marlin couchant on a field of dollar signs, which floated on little wavy lines that looked like water. At the bottom of the escutcheon was a simple motto, stitched in red: *"Il n'y a pas de petit chez soi."* Or, in my native tongue, "There's no place like home." I put it away for some future occasion.

Timing is everything.

9 ∞ Music Lovers, Arise

There are days on the water that end like a gentle benediction. Peace comes dropping slow from the haze of twilight, and the restless gulls cease tracing circles in the sky. A tender zephyr soothes the sea and bestows on it serenity.

The sailor seeks the comfort of his waiting bunk, and all around him are the sounds that lull the night. The muffled creaking of his stalwart planks. The muted voices of the lines that hold his boat secure. The liquid cadence of water lapping at his hull. The far-off chiming of a channel buoy. And like a cradle touched by loving hands, his vessel rocks in rhythm with the placid sea. Then in comes sleep on tiptoe, unbidden and unwooed.

Tell this to your insomniac friends onshore. Tell it to those landlocked masses yearning to be free. Tell it to the judge. Tell it to the Marines. But don't ever tell it to me!

Anyone who sleeps well on a boat is either drugged, desensitized, or deceased. An endless concert of creaking, groaning, sloshing, squeaking, turns the hours between dusk and dawn into a witches' sabbath of gibbering things that go bump in the night. An anchor line will rasp against its metal hawsehole with maniacal monotony. If there occurs a moment's silence, the bilge pump rushes in to fill that void with thumping, grinding, self-importance. The generator goes on and off with willful bursts of unsolicited mechanical efficiency. Water splashing against a bulkhead is endowed with a mighty power of suggestion, to which children are particularly susceptible. They are up and down every hour, weaving and wobbling their way to the toilet. And if there is any sound more obscene than the greedy sucking of an electric head, it is the choking, reluctant gargle of a hand-pumped convenience.

And inevitably, as night follows day, a visit to the galley sink follows the session in the bathroom. Water taps flood open with a great whoosh of air, and a clunking protest wells up from the pipes below. Thirst temporarily quenched, the little night crawlers retreat back into their bunks. If you're lucky, they will remember not to try to weasel in between the sheets. Normal sleeping practices are not applicable in this environment. The two V-shaped pads, tapering down to a lopped-off, slanted apex lie rigidly atop unyielding wooden shelves. Conventional techniques of bed-making are rendered inoperable. There is no way to smooth out sheets and tuck in blankets. Any attempt to do so results in a mare's nest of tangled lumps and clammy linen, too formidable a mess to face come morning.

I solved the problem by dressing the children in heavy ski suits and ordering them to sleep on top of their berths. Someday, this deprivation of their ritual tucking-in may result in psychological disaster. Let them lie on some future couch and explain why they hate their mother. In the meantime, I told them, we were all in the same boat together.

Yet a night at anchor is tranquil compared with a night at a marina dock. Magnify the noises of a single boat one hundred times. Multiply by twice as much the stuff ejected from its waste pipes. Then, in the swill of the night, add the departure and return of one inevitable clown, hell-bent on a nocturnal fishing expedition. Ye Completely Idiotic Angler, he barrels in and out of the harbor, throttles wide open, setting up a chain reaction that sends every dockside boat lunging and lurching at its lines like a maddened bronco. Imagine all this, and you begin to get the picture.

Better still, try to remember the pictures we were shown in school of the Chinese junks and sampans huddled together on the unspeakable waters of the Orient. Remember how those miserable communities, floating on the squalid rivers and estuaries of a faraway land, exemplified for us the quaint but horribly unsanitary and impoverished life-styles of places non-American? Well, East and West have finally met in the boatyards of these United States. And the Yangtze River runs through Yankee Harbor.

Some people don't see it my way. Primitive types, who could sleep through the blare of doomsday's trumpets. The captain is one of those. The only time he complained was when I quietly shifted my aching bones and listed to port when I should have rolled to starboard. Then he would awake and snarl about inconsiderate clods who fancied themselves princesses with peas under their mattresses.

This was patently ridiculous. By no stretch of the imagination could that wafer-thin pallet be called a mattress, any more than the rigid plank on which it lay could be called a bed.

To me it was a rack upon which I lowered my aching body and prayed for oblivion. One night we reached a crisis. The captain was snuggled down in his berth, at peace with the world. I was preparing to retire when the boat heaved and pitched and sent me skittering into a locker door. Something unique came over me—seasickness. My stomach churned and my head reeled. I picked up the bullhorn, an instrument used to hail other boats out of earshot and obviously designed to wake the dead, leaned over the skipper's bunk, and spoke up loud and clear.

"One for the money, two for the show, three to get ready, and *ver-ti-go!*"

The recitation had a less than salutary effect. It inspired a lecture on dockside etiquette, marina protocol, disturbance of the peace, and a stern warning that people were trying to sleep.

I was past caring. What could they do to me? Cut off my daily ration of grog? Make me walk the plank? I sailed under my own flag!

I lay down and waited for the scheduled concert to commence. Ah, there it was, the downbeat! Three sharp raps as we swung against the pilings. And "Eine Kleine Knock Musik" had begun. The serenade opened with a plaintive statement from the generator section, followed almost immediately by the contrapuntal hum of the air conditioner. The halyards and the hawsers, the spring lines and the bowlines, answered with a muted vibrato, which grew in intensity as the wood group introduced a dramatic countertheme. Dock plankings scraped and scratched against their splintery pilings, and the rail-hung bumpers throbbed against them with a variation in a minor key. All instruments were playing in unison until a subsidiary figure, scored for bilge pumps and toilets, interwove itself into the orchestral fabric. *Poco sostenuto* became *loco crescendo*, and thumping timpani rose in a thundering expression of headlong abandonment. It was a familiar piece of orchestration, basically a theme and variation structure interspersed with fugal episodes.

What I waited for now was the solo cadenza, which I knew would appear at some point in the symphony's development.

This instrumental recitative took many forms. Sometimes it consisted of a marital mutiny aboard a neighboring boat. Other times, it was the dissonant chorale of midnight revelers returning from a landside orgy. Often it was the pitiful wail of an alienated child, longing for his crib back home. Or the yelping of a dog, poor deck-bound creature, maddened by the sound and smell of sleek fat wharf rats forever out of reach.

But that particular night's cadenza was a passage of virtuoso proportions performed by a trio of wee-hour fishermen who reentered the harbor with the thrust of Dewey at Manila Bay. Coughing and barking in ear-splitting staccato bursts, their outboard motors churned into the channel. And in their wake came a great heaving and groaning as the entire flotilla rocked and reared against its moorings. In my galley I heard the coffeepot, ready with the morning's brew, rise and crash and bounce off the stove onto the deck. Fore and aft the watch dogs howled in full-throated outrage, and a baby screamed in protest. Next to us a light flashed on in a trim boat named *El Syd*, and a bellow of pure hatred rang out across her bow.

"You stinkin', bloody bastards! I'm gonna kill you!"

There was a thud as *El Syd*'s captain hit the dock and his pounding footsteps thundered as he took off in hot pursuit.

"*Vaya con Dios, Amigo El Syd,*" I whispered. "May all the saints smile on your quest."

All in all, it was one of our better nights at sea. Not atypical, just more interesting.

The captain of the *Marlyn* slept right through the entire concert.

10 ∞ Sinking in the Rain

There is no doubt that boatmen are a fraternity of free spirits.

Maybe too free. Seldom have so many known so little and dared so much. Most lawful activities, whose pursuit poses danger to the general public, require of their practitioners some training and proof of official sanction.

A license is needed to sell beer, real estate, or insurance; to be a hairdresser, a plumber, electrician, or chiropractor. One must pass a test in order to drive a car, fly a plane, operate a pushcart, or pilot a horse and buggy around the park.

But any clown with the mechanical know-how of an Australian aborigine and the sea savvy of a mountain goat can buy a twenty-ton boat with 250 horsepower engines, load it to the gunnels with friends, relations, and high-octane gasoline, and assume the cloak of Christopher Columbus! The only thing he must do is register his boat with the state and get his number up on the bow. The fact that everybody's number might soon be up arouses no official interest at all.

It's rather like licensing the plumber's wrench and trusting that the man, by instinct, knows the difference between the water pipe and the gas line.

The Power Squadron, bless its red, white, and blue ensign, does its best to bring order out of chaos. The Coast Guard stands by to pick up the pieces. Their logs are a saga of the disasters of amateur sailors, who would rather die than be called chickens of the sea.

Take our friend Simon B. Muse, a gentleman and sometime scholar. Good companion, gracious host, skilled fisherman, Falstaffian imbiber, and a menace on the high seas. Simon, Marlo always claimed, went out only when small-craft warnings were up. His friends referred to him, accurately enough, as the "Coast Card."

Simon was like the eye of a hurricane—a center of dead calm surrounded by turbulence. You were apt to watch his control in a crisis with such stunned reverence that you forgot it was he who had precipitated the whole bloody mess in the first place. Like the day he sank his third boat. It was a day I shall long remember.

The captain came home one Friday evening, having fought the battle of Madison Avenue all week with yeoman fortitude, and announced that we were going away for the weekend on a fishing trip.

Fine, I said to myself. All I have to do is find someone to take care of the children, stock up the house with groceries, cancel one wedding, one dinner engagement, and make peace with the offended parties.

When a soldier is home on leave, one tries to accommodate him.

"Where are we going?" I asked.

"Up to Simon's," he answered.

"You've got to be kidding!" I said. "Why?"

"He's invited us a dozen times. I can't say no again."

"If someone invited you a thousand times to join him in a leaky barrel going over Niagara Falls, would you go?"

"Simon's a nice guy," he said.

"So's the village idiot. What do you say we invite him to dinner."

"Simon's a very good friend," he said.

"So? You owe him friendship and goodwill. Not your life."

"Simon is a client," he said.

"What time are we leaving?" I asked.

The captain had invoked the sacred word. Simon was not merely a client. He was an important client. He bought television shows. But no show he bought boasted characters more dramatic, more flamboyant, more consistent, than Simon himself.

The house he lived in, for example, way up on a Connecticut shore, was a weather-beaten testament to Simon's affinity for the sea. It had a captain's walk outside the second floor that was dominated by a ghastly old ship's figurehead whose bulbous, unyielding breasts jutted out toward the sea with a hideous wooden arrogance. The windows were always rheumy with windblown salt spray, and at low tide there was the inescapable stench of overripe mollusks and rotting seaweed.

Inside there were coffee tables made of ships' wheels, lamps made of sextants and compasses, beds made like bunks, prints of old fighting ships on the walls.

And then there was Samantha, Simon's wife, who was allergic to fish, loved the mountains, and hated the sea. She wouldn't even put salt on her eggs. Samantha floated through life like a Pre-Raphaelite vision, only coming down to earth when her feet touched the streets of Manhattan.

When we got to Simon's house on Saturday morning we stowed our gear in one of the bunk bedrooms. In my house you would have put your clothes away, but this was not my house. We went topside, where Simon and a group of friends and neighbors were waiting to start the day's expedition.

Once aboard Simon's boat, the *Simontha III*, we headed for the spot where the striped bass were running. The *Simontha II* had gone down to a watery grave just two months before, and this new vessel was a thirty-five foot, teak-decked, completely equipped sport fisherman.

Marlo looked her over with loving approval and congratulated Simon.

"Good, safe, sturdy boat," he said.

"A boat is as good, safe, and sturdy as its captain," I said.

"Ah, come on," he coaxed. "Try to enjoy yourself."

"Oh, I will!" I promised. "I do! I love life! That's my problem."

"How's that a problem?" he demanded.

"I'm just too young to die and leave it all!"

Unfortunately, this was not the moment for tender comfort and understanding. As if on signal, all the fish began biting at once. The fishermen were hysterical with joy. There was lots of action for a couple of hours, and the *Simontha III* began to smell like the Fulton Street Fish Market at the end of a busy Friday.

After a while the slaughter tapered off and things became quiet. Simon decided to move to more fertile ground and headed for a spot near a rock ledge where stripers were known to congregate.

Suddenly, with a sickening lurch and a crunching shudder, the boat came to an abrupt halt. Simon had run her up on the reef. He customarily ignored tides, currents, wind drift, running time, and anything else he couldn't actually see. He was the kind of navigator who never took a fix, just got into one. But with his customary aplomb, Simon calmed his guests, revved up his motors, backed off the rocks, and laughingly assured us that his bottom needed scraping anyway.

I caught the captain's eye and murmured something to the effect that Simon's bottom could take care of itself. It was Simon's head that was in trouble. It needed shrinking.

The captain didn't listen and neither did anybody else. Everybody was busy counting the day's haul, and Simon was a hero.

That night we had a big, old-fashioned fish fry. Samantha had disappeared. Simon was busy mixing tankards of navy grog at the bar, and the captain was exchanging lies with several other mariners. The situation left something to be desired, as there was only one other person to get the fish ready to fry.

After an indecent interval, the captain realized somebody was missing and wandered into the kitchen.

"What're you doing?" he asked.

Anybody with one eye in his head could see what I was doing. I gave him what I hoped was a fishy stare.

"See the nice lady," I said. "What is the nice lady doing? She is having a good time. She is at a party! See how pretty she is dressed. She is wearing sequins. See how they glitter! See how they shine! Isn't the nice lady lucky?"

I held up my arms, which were covered with fish scales, and waved a bloody knife.

"Now get out of here before the nice lady goes entirely berserk!"

He did. He also made amends later. He ate four big pieces of fish to show me how he appreciated my efforts.

Simon shooed everybody out by nine o'clock because the next morning at five the four of us were going to head for the blue water, where the tuna were running out past Montauk Point.

I could hardly wait for dawn. I had never cleaned a tuna. Maybe we'd be lucky and I'd get a chance to try.

Sure enough, at five-thirty on Sunday morning we were on our way. By noon we were out in the deeps with everybody happy as clams. Samantha was doing what she enjoyed most, sleeping belowdecks while the waves rocked her into oblivion. My captain was stretched out on the foredeck, sunning himself into a gleaming bronze. I was working on the Sunday crossword puzzle, a weekly ritual that I pursue with all the fervor of a fanatic.

Simon was high, in more ways than one, up on his flying bridge with a gallon of steaming black coffee and Irish whiskey mixed in equal proportions. In his pocket was a bag of lump sugar, a piece of which Simon held between his teeth as he sipped his brew. On either side of the bridge his outriggers trailed in the water, loaded for tuna.

Meanwhile, as I found out later, back in the cabin Samantha wasn't resting as well as usual. She had a recurring dream. In it she was seated at her regular table at "21," all dressed up in a low-cut gown, while a waiter persistently poured a tray of dry martinis down her back. The fantasy was so real she woke up with the conviction that her arm, which had been dangling over the side of the bunk, was wet to the elbow. She raised the arm and sniffed it. She lifted her hand and licked it. Now if there is one thing Samantha knows, it is the smell and taste of a martini.

After a moment's thought she got up and sloshed her way to the deck, where a steady rain was falling.

"Simon," we heard her call up to the bridge, "do you think there should be two feet of water in the cabin?"

"Definitely not!" said Simon.

"Well, there is!" said Samantha.

At that instant the line on the port rigger snapped out like a whiplash, the reel spun, and Simon yelled.

"It's a big one!"

He spit the sugar out from between his teeth, cut the engines, and grabbed the rod.

But Samantha had a one-track mind.

"What'll I do?" she screamed.

Simon, the imperturbable, was ready with the answers.

"Get Marlo," he said.

She didn't have to. My husband, the captain, was already in the pilothouse, switching on the auxiliary bilge pump, while he issued a few orders of his own.

To Samantha he said, "Call the Coast Guard!"

To me he said, "Get out the life preservers!"

To Simon he said, "Help me lower the dink!"

What he said to himself, I can only guess.

Samantha said, "What should I tell them?"

I said, "Where the hell are they?"

Simon said, "I'll bet this baby weighs fifteen hundred pounds!"

To Samantha he said, "Tell 'em this is a May Day!"

To me he said, "Look for them!"

To Simon he said, "Get the hell off that bridge, you clown, or the fish'll be using you for bait!"

We were extremely busy for a few minutes, Simon being the busiest of all. He fought that fish.

He fought it while Marlo lowered the dinghy. While Samantha tearfully explained to the Coast Guard that nobody had the vaguest idea where we were. While I found the life preservers safely tucked away out of sight behind a case of beer. He fought that tuna while he climbed down from the flying bridge, while he remembered to snatch up a gaff, while he lowered himself into that miserable dinghy. He fought it while the captain and I climbed into one of those inflatable navy rafts that by the grace of God, because it couldn't have been Simon's doing, somebody had put aboard the boat.

He fought it while Samantha, with a particularly smug expression, watched *Simontha III* sink slowly down to the bottom.

By the time the rescue squad reached us, he had fought

that leviathan to a standstill. He had plenty of time in which to do it, of course. You just can't call the Coast Guard and say, "Come get us."

The sporting thing is to give them some little clue about where to look. But Simon made no apologies. He ascribed all catastrophes to malignant fate, hostile chance, or sheer accident. The only concession he made to personal liability was to remark that he must have scraped the ledge, the day before, harder than he thought or there wouldn't have been such a big hole in the bottom of his boat. Even then, he managed to imply that the goddamned rocks should never have been there in the first place.

Simon set two records that year. He caught the biggest tuna ever landed from the smallest boat and was the only sailor on Long Island Sound who managed to sink two cabin cruisers in as many boating seasons. The yachting fraternity called the incident heroic. The long-suffering Coast Guard called it another Simon-pure disaster.

11 ∞ Bali Hi — and Belly Up

Included in my log of the seafaring idiots I have known and regretted, there stands one whose name leads all the rest. Rockwell Andrew Rhodes, a prominent television vice-president of "Our Network." Along with other occupational hazards, he shared with his colleagues a padded expense account, suits from Brooks Brothers with no padding, incipient ulcers, and the dream called "Someday I'll Get Out of This Rat Race and Live a Little."

Rocky Rhodes's dream was a model of classic purity. It embraced a palm-fringed tropical island, Caribbean skies, fish leaping in a blue lagoon, white sands, and dusky natives cracking open his coconuts.

The major difference between Rocky and the rest of the dreamers was that he was a boat nut. Ergo, a man of action. He actually went out, found his place in the sun, and made a down payment on it. Along Madison Avenue, Rocky Rhodes began to enjoy a reputation as a latter-day Thoreau. The only reason he had not said his final farewells to Manhattan was that his expense account, as yet, was not elastic enough to stretch over an entire private island.

The opportunity to remedy this situation knocked on his door one day in the form of a big industrialist from the Midwest. This 250-pound giant of industry, Mr. Tyrone Coon, was an ardent and dedicated fisherman who was fascinated with Rocky's tales of the South Atlantic. He had been flirting with the idea of sponsoring one of Rocky's programs, a canine epic that was a dog in every sense of the word.

Rocky claimed it was a natural because Ty Coon was the biggest manufacturer of pet food in America. The bait Rocky dangled in front of the prospective client was slightly rotten but wrapped in a lovely package. He proposed a week's midwinter holiday, along with Marlo and me, at his personal Shangri-la. Included in the party was the lady Rocky had been escorting for a long time, whom he intended to marry someday only if he couldn't avoid it.

The reason he invited us was perfectly clear. We were friends. Also, Marlo was a fellow boat owner and thereby qualified for the expedition. What's more, Rocky was going to need somebody who could pull his lousy show together before it set television back more than a few years. I suspect that the last reason was the main one.

Over a table at Sardi's, Rocky outlined a week in paradise. Long, sunny days, with big fish practically jumping into the boat. A curving beach that swung in a lazy crescent against the foaming curl of the water. Feathered tops of palm trees leaning toward the turquoise seas like a jade necklace around the white throat of sand. Sunsets filled with the scent of banyan, jasmine and wisteria, while the waters turned into a sheet of rippled copper. And in between time, armed with frosted glasses of Jamaican rum and pineapple juice, they could iron out the minor problems of the show.

✦ ✦ ✦

It was a beautiful script. The client could land his fish. Rocky could land his client. The swindle sheet could be loaded way above the cargo line. And everybody could get a vacation for nothing. A kind of Rhodes scholarship.

The night before we were to leave I asked the captain, "What shall I take?"

"What do you mean, 'What shall you take?' "

"I mean what clothes should I take? What should I wear on the plane?"

"Where do you think you're going? To an embassy dinner in Rome?"

"Why do you always answer a question with a question? What is this Socratic method of discourse?"

"You're going fishing on a boat. Wear what you usually wear. Slacks, sneakers. Take a bathing suit, a sweater and a raincoat. What else could you possibly need?"

I thought it over.

"O.K. Do you think I ought to get my hair done?"

He opened his mouth, but I stopped him.

"Forget it. Strike the question from the record. It was immaterial, incompetent, and irreverent."

"You mean irrelevant."

"I meant exactly what I said!"

Heaven forfend that mere feminine vanity should sully the holy world of those who challenge the sea!

It was a gala group that boarded a jet bound for the Virgin Islands that snowy Friday morning. Five happy people filled with the joy of living and one absolutely miserable female.

I had never met Rocky's girlfriend or Mrs. Coon before, but one look and I knew them. They were members of that Olympian society who people the pages of *Vogue* and *Harper's Bazaar*. The women who march to the beat of fashion's drummer and are photographed in front of their personal El Grecos in their personal townhouses and country châteaus.

There I was in my slacks and loafers, raincoat slung debonairly over my arm, short-cropped hair uncoiffed and unattended. And there they were—mink coats casually draped over their casual imported Italian knits, Pucci scarves and Gucci handbags, sporting just the chic amount of chunky gold jewelry, clinging daintily to their elegant cosmetic cases. Almost every woman in the world has at some time had a similar experience, and she will know how I felt. To put it simply, like a slob.

We settled down in the plane, along with hordes of matched luggage, three transistor radios, a typewriter, a portable tape recorder, a small record player, a case of dance records (Caribbean tempos), scuba gear, cameras, two hair dryers, and a battery-operated ice crusher.

The captain asked me why I was so quiet, but I didn't answer. I was very busy hating him. Also, I was occupied with a little personal therapy based on the application of positive thinking.

"Take stock," I told myself. "What have they got that you haven't got? Nothing. What have you got that they haven't got? Plenty! My vocabulary, for one thing. I'll bet neither of those two bedecked broads knows what an ichthyologist is, for instance. My youth, comparatively speaking. They've got to be at least ten years older than I am. My husband, brute though he is. Take a look at him. Take a look at their men. Come right down to it, one of them hasn't even got a husband, and Lord knows she's tried."

I was beginning to feel better.

"So they look gorgeous. So what? So would I if I had time to think about it. So they've got clothes. So what else is new? I've got a house in the country. And two fantastic children. And a beautiful boat. With beautiful equipment, practically a yacht is what it is. With practically a yacht's upkeep! That's why I've got stainless steel and they've got gold trinkets. And that's why I've got a deck-to-galley carpet and they've got mink coats. Whose fault is that, I ask you!"

I glared at the captain, but he didn't notice, as he was busy laughing it up with our four companions. They noticed nothing because included in their impedimenta was a simply darling, completely stocked bar that fitted into a simply divine piece of hand luggage. Their gay chatter and clever repartee had risen to a glorious pitch as the morning wore on. By the time the plane set down in St. Thomas, everything was strictly *La Vie en Rose*. For them.

Just before we landed, Rocky explained the logistics of the next few hours. He had cabled ahead, with true executive dispatch, and all signals were *go!* The local taxi boat was to take the five of us to his island. This was the best way, he said, because his own boat, which was only twenty-three feet long, would be overladen with six passengers, six tons of luggage, and six days' worth of eatables and potables. Thus everybody, with no delay, could set out unencumbered.

Rocky himself would gather up all the necessities, from caviar to canned crepes suzette. He would stow them, along with the baggage, fishing tanks full of fresh bait, blocks of ice under tarpaulin, and meet us on the island an hour or so later. The taxi had been alerted to stand by, the dusky natives to ready up the house, and the Almighty to get the weather on the beam.

So out they trouped, down to the dock, impeccably chic, ineffably sophisticated, impossibly gay. Rocky led the parade.

"Come on, kiddies," he called cheerfully. "All aboard!"

And then the dawn began to break. Mrs. Coon caught one of her elegant high-heeled shoes in a crack on the dock and went down on one knee, ripping her nylon stockings. Rocky's girlfriend bent down to help her, and the lovely Pucci scarf flew off into the water. On its way it snagged one earring, which rolled with utter precision right between two planks and out of sight. Then Mr. Coon gazed with horrified disbelief at the taxi boat toward which Rocky was herding them.

"You propose to take us out there in this?" he barked, pointing to the sea.

His spouse froze by his side. "Not me!" she shrieked.

Rocky's girlfriend was torn between loyalty to Rocky and her sense of the appropriate. Rocky lost. She backed away and told him, "Not on your life, lover!"

The captain and I looked at each other. We'd seen this kind of panic before. We call it the landlubber's lament, the general refrain of which is, "Get me outa here!"

I will say that the waiting taxi was a pathetic little underslung dory, paint-peeled and leprous-looking, with open benches and an antiquated little motor amidships. Our host laughingly poopoohed their fears.

"Ty, baby, this taxi's been ferrying people back and forth to the out islands for twenty-five years. It's the Wells Fargo of the Caribbean. Aunty Quarrie knows every drop of water from here to Puerto Rico."

"My God!" said Ty Coon, looking at the taxi driver. "It's a woman."

"How can you tell the sex of a mummy?" hissed his wife.

The captain jumped into the breach.

"It's perfectly safe," he told them. "The water's like glass."

He held out his hand to Mrs. Coon, who looked at it as if it were a snake. I was feeling better and better, and my estimation of the captain was rising like a barometer after a storm. The chic had become the chickens. With the grace of a gazelle I leaped into the boat, my sneaker-clad feet making a perfect landing, my slacks-clad legs unimpeded and free. It was a highly stylish maneuver.

"Either get in or take the next plane back," I said. "But remember, it's snowing in New York."

The captain looked at me with obvious admiration. "She's right," he told them. "Let me help you."

Coaxing the women in their garters and girdles and tight skirts into the taxi took a bit of doing. Getting the full tonnage of Mr. Coon into the exact center of the little craft took even more dexterity. One centimeter off balance toward the bow or stern and we would have owed Aunty a new rapid transit. Rocky stood on the dock, mink coats draped over one arm, waving a bon voyage and shouting words of encouragement.

Aunty peered at the women silently, like an anthropologist studying a lower group of primates. She worked her gums, spat into the water, started her engine, and headed seaward.

It was a beautiful, glorious day. A tropical breeze wafted across my face and brought the scent of some sweet and improbable flower. As for the water, it sparkled like a diamond-studded azure field. You'd never have known it, watching the zombies, who sat rigid, resentful, and ridiculous.

After an uneventful hour or so, Mrs. Coon came to life.

"I have to go to the ladies room," she announced.

"Marlo," I asked, "do you know which way it is to the ladies room?"

He shook his head solemnly.

"Aunty, do you know which way it is to the ladies room?"

She spat into the ocean. I turned back to Mrs. Coon.

"I'm so sorry. Nobody seems to know. But I have a suggestion."

And I proceeded to explain the obvious. How a nimble female can balance herself on the gunnels, and so forth. She listened with growing horror.

"I'll wait," she announced with lofty martyrdom.

"You do that," I agreed.

All this time, Aunty Quarrie hadn't said one word. Suddenly she raised a skinny arm and pointed straight ahead.

There it was. A little jewel of an island. Small waves raced toward its shore, tiny white horses with streaming manes. An opalescent beach, where surely no man had ever set foot before, welcomed the sailor home from the sea. If a Spanish galleon, sails pregnant with wind, had appeared on the horizon, her thrusting bow rising to meet the rolling waters, I wouldn't have been a bit surprised.

Neither was I surprised by the reaction of our companions. They looked where I looked, and all they saw was Rocky's weather-beaten, sun-bleached little cottage high on a bluff, modestly holding back the wilderness. In voices of disbelief and disgust, they all spoke simultaneously.

"That's Rocky's house?"

I knew what they had pictured. A gleaming Caribbean plantation manor with red-tile roofs and second-story balconies, with vine-covered porticoes and wide verandas and majestic chimneys, and all that romantic nineteenth-century jazz they'd seen in the movies.

"You were expecting maybe the Carib Hilton?" I asked.

We were about thirty yards from shore when Aunty cut her motors, pointed to the water and opened her mouth.

"Out!" she said. "You get out here."

"What the flaming hell do you mean?" bellowed Ty Coon.

"In these clothes?" screamed Rocky's girlfriend. "That crazy savage is crazy!"

"I won't! I simply won't!" Mrs. Coon threatened her husband. "I'll stay here until hell freezes over! Who knows what's lurking down in that water?"

They could have saved their breath.

"Sandbar," Aunty gestured toward the beach. "Too shallow for boat. Just right for walking. Dock gone. Big hurricane blowed it away. Last September."

"Then we'll wait right here!" Mr. Coon said firmly. "Right here!"

Aunty spat over the side.

"No can do," she said. "I got two-hour trip to other islan'. Stay there two days. Goobye."

She squinted into the sun.

"Late now," she grunted and started her engine.

So I jumped over the side.

"Come on," I urged Mrs. Coon. "Here's your chance. This is God's great, big, self-flushing outdoor privy!"

She clutched her Gucci handbag as if it were the only thing that stood between her and eternity.

"Never!" she yelled. "I can't swim! I'll drown!"

"In four feet of water?" I yelled back. "What are you afraid of? Icebergs?"

"She's right," said the captain, which made this a red-letter day. He'd said it twice in two hours!

Taking charge, he persuaded them out of the boat amid wails and lamentations. Standing thigh-deep in the water, he lifted and tugged and exhorted.

"Pretend you're getting out of a taxi on Fifty-second Street," I suggested. "Give the nice doorman your hand. He'll help you."

Ty Coon went over the side, landed on all fours, and came up sputtering. We were lucky he didn't cause a tidal wave.

With the captain leading the way they started walking, bouffant hairdos, imported suits, shoes in hand. I brought up the rear, shouting my own brand of encouragement. In spite of the fact that wool knits, girdles, clinging skirts, white linen planter's suits, and Leica cameras do not take kindly to ocean bathing, things went relatively well. Until we came to a spot where the sandbar sloped down a couple of feet before it came up again.

The men found themselves up to their chins, but the ladies found themselves in a completely subaqueous world. They couldn't cope. By the time Marlo had rescued them, and led them to shore, Mrs. Coon was hysterical. Rocky's girlfriend had lost her bag, her shoes, and her other earring. Mr. Coon lay on the sand like a beached whale. The chic coiffures of both ladies had suffered a drastic change. Their hair draggled down their necks, a gummy mass of salt and lacquer. I found myself beginning to feel sorry for them but managed to resist the impulse by recalling how they had looked at me at the airport. The message they had tacitly passed between them took no psychic to divine.

"What in God's name does he see in her?"

"Maybe she inherited money."

"Maybe. It's unbelievable. Such a gorgeous, bright man!"

That gorgeous, bright man was beginning to look grim as he bent over Mrs. Coon, who lay screaming on the sand.

"My foot! My foot! A shark bit my foot!"

"Nothing bit your foot," he snapped. "You scraped it on a rock."

"Come now, fellow Americans," I said. "Is this the attitude our forefathers displayed when they crossed a continent and opened up the West for us future generations?"

The captain turned to me.

"Wait here with these Americans. I'll run up to the house and get help."

He was back in ten minutes, bearing ill tidings. Not only was no one there, but the place had been battened down with steel hurricane shutters. Without tools there wasn't a crack or cranny we could break into.

By this time the sun was lowering over the yardarm. The temperature had dropped about twenty degrees, and a stiff wind was blowing in from the sea. Our companions were wet and sandy, cold and tired, and starving. Rocky's girlfriend started to shiver and sneeze, but no one could even produce a usable handkerchief. I gave her my Macy's raincoat.

The captain cracked open a few fallen coconuts.

"Eat these," he advised. "Sorry it isn't filet mignon."

Nothing helped. All they could do was huddle on the beach and wait for Rocky to come—so they could kill him.

That gentleman, however, needed no help in bringing about his own demise, because for once he had conscientiously followed the safety rules laid down by the Coast Guard. Ever aware of the danger of trapped gas fumes, they urged thorough ventilation before a boat gets under way—especially a boat that has been closed for a length of time.

So after stowing everything in the forward cabin, Rocky opened the bow hatch to let the air course through, climbed up on his fishing tower, and took off.

Out in the open water a real wind sprang up, and the Caribbean began to act like the North Atlantic. Rocky had his hands full. He also had a boat full—of seawater. He didn't realize it until his engine conked out and he drifted over a coral reef and tore a man-sized hole in his bottom. When he went below to investigate, the ocean was pouring into the open hatch and the open bottom, the bilges were full beyond pumping, and the accumulated gear was under two feet of brine.

Rocky rushed up on deck and started to scream. When that proved of no avail, he started to pray. The sun was sinking. So was his boat. Then, like an answer from heaven, he heard a voice call.

"You in trouble, boss?"

Below him he saw a little homemade dory with a little one-cylinder motor manned by a little boy who had the biggest grin that ever spread sunshine across a little brown face.

When Rocky and his rescuer finally putt-putted into the island, his former friends were on their feet to greet him. At first he tried to explain and apologize. Then he got into the spirit of the thing and began to wave his arms and scream like the rest.

Withdrawing from the arena, the captain pulled out a water-soaked bill from his wallet and gave it to the little one-man rescue squadron.

"Can you get word to somebody to come out here and get us?" he asked.

"Yeah, boss. When you want?"

The captain looked at the savage foursome. He looked at the sky. There was a full moon, and it made a path of silver from the water's edge to the horizon. The white beach beckoned, and in the silent brush a few night birds called gently to each other.

"Tomorrow morning will do, son," said my brave and fearless leader.

Grinning, he turned to me.

"Don't you think a night on the beach will do 'em all good?" he asked.

"Frankly," I answered, "I'm not so much interested in doing them good as doing them in for good."

We started to walk along the sand.

"The time has come," the captain said, "to talk of many things."

"Like ships and shoes?" I began to laugh. "That's very appropriate."

"Like the fact that I think you're terrific," he said.

I nodded.

"And that I'm very proud of you."

I nodded again.

"And that I love you."

"You took the words out of my mouth," I said. "And may I add that you are no longer to be referred to as the captain? From now on, henceforth and forever more, you are promoted to the rank of admiral of the fleet. And that's official!"

As for Rocky, he is still paying for those mink coats and sets of matched luggage. But he is not too crushed. For one thing, he no longer has to worry about marrying the girlfriend. She wouldn't have him if he were the last man alive on a deserted island. And he has managed to make a down payment on a house in New Hampshire. He's given up boating, which is a fine thing for the rest of us. He's switched from seas to skis, and rumor has it that he's already zooming down the slopes like a pro. He uses words like sitz, mark, slalom, wedel, and schuss. So long, Sailor! What's new, Schussy Cat?

12 ∞ Swede-Hearts No More

The mishaps of recreation boaters range from the catastrophic to the comic. But not all of them can be blamed on the caprices of that ol' debbil sea. There have been plenty of misadventures on lakes, too. We can attest to one.

It started with an invitation from Mr. Inger Ingberg, an advertising client. One of the last of the genuine, old-fashioned empire builders, he had come to these shores from Norway as a small boy and wrested a fortune from the forests of our Northwest.

We called him Inger Iceberg because two thirds of what he thought was hidden beneath the surface, and the visible part could freeze you to death with an ice-blue glance.

Mr. I. had homes all over the United States, but his favorite was a summer lodge in northern Minnesota. Built on a rocky tor in the middle of a lake, it was ten miles by water from the town of International Falls. That little outpost enjoys the lowest temperatures of any city within our continental limits and for two thirds of the year is under a glacier. A perfect setting for a descendant of the foraging Norsemen.

We got to Mr. I's island by plane, train, car, and boat. Even in the summer, the border country is formidable, with endless waters, tall timber, and jagged rocks. The lodge itself, high on a cliff, could have been the local hangout of the old Norse gods. We were ushered into the main hall, a mammoth room with half-timbered vaulted ceiling, stone walls, and a baronial fireplace ablaze against the chill of a late August night. On the walls were mementos of the local hunt—bear, deer, moose, elk, wolf, and bobcat—all staring with glassy eyes at the revelry below.

Clustered around a lavish smorgasbord were more of our host's trophies, stuffed but not yet mounted. In the group were his son and grandson by a turn-of-the-century marriage. An adopted daughter and her child from his middle matrimonial venture. His current spouse with a tow-headed little boy who had been delivered, on approval, for possible adoption. The imported game, besides us, consisted of three corporate heads of subsidiary companies and their wives, and his favorite nephew, Lief, an arrogant young giant visiting from Sweden.

In the morning the entire assemblage was to board Mr. I's seventy-five-foot yacht and travel north to an island he owned but had never visited. He had bought it, sight unseen, because, according to native lore, it was the site of a Viking expedition that had sailed down from Hudson Bay and landed there in the eleventh century. Ancient stone mooring posts with iron hawser rings supposedly marked a cove, and the ruins of a stone tower still remained somewhere on that island. To a thwarted archaeologist like me, a legend is always truth undiscovered. I was all excitement.

At dawn we met at the boathouse—a dock-lined shelter carved out of a cliff like the hall of the Mountain King. Loaded aboard were tents, sleeping bags, blankets, cooking gear, boots, axes, lanterns, and enough equipment for sixteen adults and two children. Most important of all was a huge iron caldron, filled to the brim with a special Scandinavian stew that had been simmering in the castle kitchens for twenty-four hours.

At the wheel was Lief, the taciturn blond giant from the fjords, who had proudly proclaimed his lifelong experience at sea. Only the call of the loons and the purr of the motors broke the stillness until at four o'clock we sighted Iceberg's island, as much to Lief's surprise as ours, I think. A boulder-strewn beach curved down to a cove, and dark behind it rose the primeval forest. Two serfs lowered the motor dinghy and began to set up camp onshore. Soon a fire was crackling, the pot was hung over it, tents were pitched, and the passengers were relayed in pairs to land. I have never seen such beautiful serenity.

The tang of pine and bracken mingled with the smell of that beautiful stew, and when the dinner call came, we rushed like wolves to fill our plates.

I heaped mine like a mountain, sat down on a flat ledge, and raised the first succulent mouthful. Halfway to my mouth, I stopped. The thing was moving! I looked down at the plate, and the rich brown gravy had turned to a scummy black. I looked up, and the sky was filled with a buzzing cloud of flying mosquitoes!

The aromatic vat had sent out signals just at feeding time, and they descended on that beach like a plague. What they had fed on for centuries, I don't know. But now they had discovered meat, and soon it didn't matter whether it was cooked or living flesh. In one minute my arms were as fuzzy as my dinner.

I heard Mr. I's corporation voice issue orders above the whir of a billion wings.

"Svenson! Dump the food in the lake! Olaf, untie the dinghy and start the engine. Lief, get the women and children in the lake up to their chins! Jens, out to the yacht and rev up the motors. Abandon everything onshore! Those who can't swim, wait in the water till you are picked up. The rest, swim for it! Take the children first."

With cursing and crying and general confusion, we plunged into the water, where a cloud of steam marked the last resting place of that wonderful Scandinavian stew. Since the cruiser was anchored a full quarter mile out, it was quite a swim with all our clothes on.

Once everyone was safely on board, we hauled anchor and started home, but one small problem faced us. We were in the middle of a labyrinth of small islands, surrounded by shallow water full of jutting rocks and invisible ledges. To navigate by daylight was one thing. To find the channels by night was something else, and Lief decided to head in a general direction and rely on the fathometer.

Suddenly the voice of my captain rose loud and clear. He may not have the blood of Leif Ericson in his veins, but he has something better—two years of Power Squadron under his belt!

"We will not rely on the fathometer!" he barked.

There was a moment of frozen silence.

Mr. I spoke. "Why not, sir! I paid three hundred and fifty dollars for that equipment, imported from Sweden!"

"Because," said Marlo, with equal cool, "unless you intend to dive for pearls, it isn't worth thirty-five cents! It will only tell you what depth is beneath. I am interested in what's ahead. By the time that gadget informs us, we won't need it. The sound of splintering wood and in-rushing water will be all the signal we need."

The chairman of the board considered.

"You have a better idea?"

"I do. We will plumb."

"Ve vill vat?" sneered Lief the Lusty.

"Plumb! Sound! Back home in Missouri, we call it Mark Twaining! Get a line, a hammer, and a flashlight!"

The boss nodded.

"He's right. Get them."

Lief got them.

"Now," said the new skipper, "tie a knot every twelve inches. Count the number of knots. Knock the head off the hammer. Tie it to the end of the line. Stand on the bow, and make like mighty Thor himself. Hurl that hammer out in front of us. When it hits bottom, count the knots. If it measures less than five feet, take soundings to port and starboard."

It took an hour and a half to grope our way back to open water. By then the Viking on the bow was too tired to move, and we didn't see Lief until he appeared just before dawn, as we approached home.

"I vill take de veel now!" he announced.

"You're *velcome* to it," said the interim captain. "Only vatch it. We've got a fast current. Don't throttle up too much when you jockey her around the cove. If you have to pull down your speed, she's liable to stall."

Every blond hair on Lief's noble head bristled.

"I do it de vay I alvays do it!"

So he gassed up the engines, jerked the boat around, lined her up with the boathouse, throttled down, and stalled his motors. Sixty-five tons of boat, out of control with plenty of momentum, headed right for the stone cliff at the back of the tunnel. In the time it takes to crack an eggshell, seventy-five feet of yacht were reduced to sixty-five feet.

By the grace of God, no one was on the bow. A stunned hush followed the crash. Mr. I. came up on deck, rested from a good night's sleep. He smiled at Lief, whose hands were still gripped tightly to the wheel.

"I take it we're home," he said.

Marlo and I left that afternoon, knowing that Lief would not only be written out of the will but his head would probably be impaled on a pike staff by morning. As we pulled away from the Minnesota Valhalla, I turned to the father of my children.

"Well, you know what I always say about the advertising business. When you take unto yourself a client, you gotta take him for better or for Norse."

"To that," he answered, "I would not even Dane to reply!"

13 ∞ Love Is Never Having to Say He's Wrong

"To every thing there is a season, a time to every purpose under the heaven." So in his wisdom spake Ecclesiastes. He might have added, "And to everything there's an exception." A boatman's passion for boating, for example.

Every year, for instance, I looked forward to that blessed interval that provided a surcease from the joys of boating. It was my favorite time—winter. Every well-ordered existence should have a plan for all seasons, and from November to April we could all live a good, healthy, indoor life. Could anything be cozier than a fire crackling on the hearth, a kettle singing on the stove, the ecstatic sound of children romping and tumbling in the snow?

I remember such a day, a real Grandma Moses picture-postcard kind of day. I was looking out of the window at the white blanket that weighed down the boughs of the pine trees, watching the silhouettes of the children as they dragged their sleds up and down the hill.

I turned to the captain. "Did you ever see anything more beautiful?"

"I feel a cold coming on," he said, sniffling. "I think I strained my back shoveling the snow. I'll have to see a doctor."

"Nonsense," I suggested. "Take an aspirin."

"Won't help."

He sagged in his chair.

"I think I'm developing rickets."

"With the food you get in this house?"

"Got nothing to do with diet," he said. "It's a lack of sunshine."

What he was really ailing from was his annual bout of cabin fever, brought on by being confined to his forty-five hundred square feet of hearth and home. I suffered more than he did, because his complaints were unending, unreasonable, and unbearable.

"Why don't we take a vacation?" I offered. "A change of place and pace."

"Impossible," he answered. "Somebody has to work to pay the bills for all this."

I could see the faint outlines of a martyr's halo glowing around his head.

The phone rang just then, which was a good thing, because I was about to say something about the cost of dry-docking the boat for five useless months.

Not wishing to break an established habit, I listened in. It was our friend Richard Tait calling from Miami Beach.

"Hello? Marlo? This is Dick. How are you, buddy?"

"Fine, pal. Just fine."

This in the mournful tones of a man who has relinquished all hold on life.

"You don't sound it. What're you doing?"

"Waiting for the ambulance to take me away. How's the weather down there?"

"Terrific. Eighty-six, and not a cloud in the sky."

"Great. Ask me how it is up here."

"Don't have to. It's twenty-nine degrees, overcast, wind from the northeast at seventeen miles per hour, barometer falling, more snow by tonight."

"How the hell do you know?" the landlocked sailor demanded.

"I checked," said his friend.

Leave it to Dick Tait. He always nailed everything down.

"That's one reason I'm calling. Figure you need a change. Get a little sunshine. Want you to come down and stay at the new house for a few days."

"Thanks, Dick, but . . ."

"Other reason is we're having a double celebration. Housewarming and boat launching. Want you to help crew for me, buddy."

"A boat launching? Since when have you been interested in boats? What'd you do, give up the horses?"

"Not at all. Just figured I needed a new hobby. Might as well take advantage of the situation. I calculate we have two hundred and twenty-one days of boating weather a year down here. Makes it worthwhile."

The captain thought it over carefully for maybe five seconds.

"We'll be there," he said firmly.

Here we go again, I said to myself. Aloud I said, "How can we make a trip in your condition?"

"I will pull myself together," the captain said staunchly.

"How many times are we going to face disaster because of your crackpot friends?" I asked him.

"But, honey," he answered. "Dick's different. He's reliable."

He had a point. Dick Tait was the richest real estate developer in Florida and its biggest landowner. His extraordinary success was not due to luck and accident. It came about because Richard knew more about land values than anyone else in the South. In his files, indexed and cross-indexed, was information about every field and swamp, every railroad siding and tank town, every water table and sandspit in the state. Accompanying those statistics was a complete dossier on the sociological, political, agricultural, and commercial potential of each area.

He applied the same method of operation to his horse farm. Dick was the first man to breed horses by computer analysis. The genetic records of his livestock went back ten generations. They were a mathematical miracle of prognosis. What's more, his horses won with astonishing regularity.

I arranged for a taxi, packed the bags, called the airport, and made reservations. I was not without a few reservations of my own. After all, a hundred times bitten, a thousand times shy.

Now I am not committed to the doctrine that advises the shoemaker to stick to his last. In a free and mobile society it is only right that people reach out, trod new paths, and live a little. On the other hand, there are very few Renaissance men running around. Men who are endowed with such grace that they can do everything well. Expertise in one field does not ensure against the possibility of making a horse's ass of oneself in another.

Nowhere is this phenomenon more prevalent than in the boating world. Give a man a deck to stride upon, and he is an instant John Paul Jones. I realized, however, that there were exceptions, and Dick Tait was one of them. He had proved it many times over.

So it was with great expectations that I deplaned at the Miami airport. Richard, impeccably turned out in yachting whites, was waiting for us in his new Maserati. I forgot to mention that he is a car buff, too, and knows all about internal combustion engines, overdrives, camshafts, and other such arcane matters.

"I can't wait till I see the new house," I told him.
"Wait'll you see the new boat!" he said.
I assured him I could wait, and he drove us to the house. Like everything Dick did, it was perfection. A neo-Venetian palace facing the sparkling waters of Biscayne Bay. An emerald lawn sloped down to a magnificent dock lined with gaily striped hitching poles and bedecked with blue-and-white cocktail tables and matching umbrellas.

Dick explained what was going to happen.

"People will begin arriving at four o'clock," he told us. "They'll mill around, have a few drinks. Anna will show them the house. Then, at five-thirty, we'll come in with the boat, surprise everybody, and have a launching party."

He pointed to a bottle of champagne, festooned with multicolored ribbons, hanging from one of the poles.

"It'll be a gas!"

"What do you mean?" I asked. "It's to be three by sea, and the rest by limousine?"

"I need you," he said. "After all, I'm relatively new at this. After the launching, we'll have dinner on the lawn, and Anna's got some strolling musicians dressed like gondoliers coming. It'll be a helluva party."

I didn't doubt it. Anna was like her husband. A perfectionist. She was a list maker. For example, she had a file on every party she'd ever given, complete with guest rosters, menus, and decorations. That way, she was never faced with the supreme embarrassment of serving the same thing twice to the same people.

All the way to the boatyard, Dick talked about his new purchase. How he'd found the best ship's architect to design it. How he'd gotten the latest electric gadgets aboard to make life easy. How he'd conducted a thorough survey before he chose a reliable builder to make it.

As we entered the yard, he wet one finger and held it out in the breeze.

"Ah," he smiled. "A good, fresh easterly wind coming up!"

An alarm bell rang somewhere in my head.

"What's so good about that?" I asked.

"Why, we'll sail in like a homing pigeon," he replied.

Pointing to his boat, he babbled, "There she is! What do you think of her?"

"May God help us!" was all I could think of.

Dick's pride and joy was thirty-five feet of sleek sailboat, with a mast that rose seventy-five feet into the stratosphere.

Even the captain looked a little bit seasick.

"She's a beauty, all right," he gulped. "But to tell the truth, Richard, I don't know much about sailboats."

"Tell him the truth, Marlo," I urged. "Tell him you don't know a damned thing about sailboats!"

Dick couldn't have cared less.

"Look," he said, "we're not making an ocean voyage. All we have to do is go across the Bay. Besides, I've done a lot of research. I read every manual I could find on the subject, and I'm familiar with all the principles involved. You know me!"

"But surely you've heard it referred to as the 'art of sailing,'" I wailed. "Nobody ever became an artist by reading a book!"

"We're wasting time," Dick said. "Let's get under way."

There was no way out. We scrambled aboard, cast off, and Dick took his station behind the wheel.

"Press the button," he told the captain. "It raises the sails electrically. No struggle."

The canvas went up, caught the wind, and snapped out like billowing balloons. We were on our way to a party. In five minutes the shore was far away and a stiff wind pushed us along at a staggering clip.

Now I want to be fair about sailboats. They are sleek and beautiful sights to see. They make no noise, and they glide silently and smoothly as a gull. There is no smell of gasoline or oil to sully the air, and no engine vibrations to shatter your nerves and churn your stomach.

And I loathe them! Their decks are always wet and slippery. Their booms swing back and forth like mad creatures bent on your destruction. They heel to port or starboard at almost ninety-degree angles. Their heavy, salt-stiffened lines and canvas will tear your arms out of their sockets, and there is never enough headroom below. You are forever clinging, stooping, dodging, or crouching. To me, Robert Fulton was a very great man.

After about forty minutes of clinging like a barnacle, I could see the Tait house on the shore. It looked most festive, what with the colored lanterns on the lawn and all the guests strolling about. I could even hear strains of music from the gondolieri on the dock.

Dick glanced at his watch.

"Exactly on time," he remarked, highly satisfied with the efficiency of the operation. "Lower the sails, Marlo. We'll come in under power."

"Aye, aye, sir," said the erstwhile captain, and he pressed the button.

Nothing happened.

"Take 'em down, buddy," urged Dick. "We're coming in fast!"

Same result.

I could see the activity at the dock more clearly now.

"Lower the friggin' sails, fella!" This time Dick screamed in mortal terror.

"It doesn't work," yelled the captain. "Bring her about!"

The helmsman swung the wheel with all his might, and the boat skidded into a gradual arc, while the canvas shipped around and the whole vessel listed to starboard until it was almost parallel to the water.

Round and round we went, in sickening circles, while the

captain struggled with the sails and poor Richard struggled with the helm. Every time we came around near shore, we waved frantically. The party people waved right back. They thought Dick was showing off, like the stunt pilots who fly upside down and execute double loops.

Our screams went unheard. The musicians were following Anna's instructions to keep things moving.

Dick pleaded with Marlo. "Take 'em down by hand, buddy!"

Marlo explained to Dick, "The lines are snarled at the top. We'd have to cut them."

Dick was amenable. "Go ahead and cut 'em!" he said.

The captain bellowed back, "With what? My teeth? You haven't even got a razor blade aboard!"

Dick looked up to the top of the mast. From where I sat, it loomed like the Eiffel Tower.

"Somebody oughta go up there and free those lines," he said.

"Well, that somebody is not me!" snarled the captain.

I did not like the way the conversation was going. Not that I believed for one moment that either of those two gallant gentlemen would have suggested that I give it a try. But years at sea have somewhat conditioned my reflexes. I removed my shoes and climbed over the rail.

"Where the blazing hell do you think you're going?" my captain shouted.

"I'm going to a party!" I yelled back, and prepared to jump.

"Watch out for barracuda!" Dick yelped, with touching concern.

"As long as you're going, bring back a knife!" the captain shouted.

"I'll consider it," I warned. "Remember, they give you thirty years for homicide in this state. No matter how justified!"

And so I jumped into beautiful Biscayne Bay, where millionaires' homes line the shores, where sumptuous yachts ride at anchor, where tropical gardens spill their lushness down to the retaining walls that hold back the sea. Where the garbage of Greater Miami collects.

The Bay is one big cesspool, filled with the debris and offal that flow in an unending stream from the homes and boats and estuaries that empty into it. The ocean has its tides, its ebbs and flows to flush it clean. The Bay has nothing. Sometimes the water is actually brown with sewage. This was one of those times. Barracuda were the least of my worries. It was the stuff that came floating by that scared me to death.

But there was nothing to do but keep putting one arm over the other until I reached the dock where the beautiful people were whooping it up. Things slithered by me that make me shiver even now. Things touched my toes and wrapped themselves around my ankles and caught in my hair. As I was swimming, a constant refrain kept beating in my head:

"Dear God! Why me? Other women go to parties. I swim to mine through a dark tunnel of slime. Other women face nothing worse than a flat tire or a burned-out toaster. Why do I face death and disaster, battle the elements, and risk life and limb? Why can some women break down and weep when they break a fingernail, while I am being brave and courageous? When did I ever say I wanted to be a pioneer mother?"

When I finally reached the dock and someone hauled me up, I looked and smelled like a creature from the lower depths.

Anna was horrified but solicitous.

"Poor, brave darling," she said. "Come right in and we'll draw you a bath."

"I need the decontamination squad first," I told her. "But what I came in for, aside from the exercise, was not a bath. For heaven's sake, go call the Coast Guard!"

I looked at the guests nibbling goodies and looking amused. Combined with what was already on top of my skin, they got under my skin. Like the citizens of ancient Rome watching gladiators hack each other to pieces, they watched the Flying Dutchmen of the Florida East Coast go round and round in futile circles. Gleeful, heartless brutes, while my poor captain, like some doomed mariner in a horror tale, spun endlessly on a ghost ship in full sail.

I felt that way until I remembered whose idea it was to come here in the first place. And who had made small of my fears and overridden my objections? And who could have been home right now, being a father to his children by helping them build a snow fort or something?

Once I had answered that basic question, I felt better. I went inside and took a bath with lots of perfumed bubbles and came down and joined the happy spectators. I filled a plate with beef Wellington and petit pois soufflé, and watched the Coast Guard maneuver itself into position to board the sailboat and reef those sails. All in all, it was a pretty good show.

The boat christening ceremony never did take place. The only thing that was launched was Anna Tait, who went into orbit like a rocket when Dick came ashore. Her schedule had not included this kind of entertainment.

The captain, when he finally hit dry land, found himself backed into a corner. I had a little speech prepared, and I proceeded to make it. Maybe he was in a weakened condition, because he listened and I spoke.

"Now hear this! Now hear this! This is your first officer speaking! We will henceforth make no entangling foreign alliances. We will not join forces with any alien naval power. We will remember that Almighty God made the land as well as the sea, for the use and enjoyment of mankind. We will engrave the following words upon our hearts and adhere to them: 'Friendship Stops at the Water's Edge!' "

He put his right hand over his heart, and his left hand up in the air.

"Amen!" he said. "And so be it!"

14 ⚓ Don't Look Now, *Marlyn,* But You've Got a Hole in Your Bottom

You can see that it's great sport for a boatman to sit in the smug harbor of his own infallibility and laugh at the antics of his fellows. But it's playing with a two-edged sword. Sooner or later everyone gets his comeuppance.

We got ours at the Power Squadron Overnight Rendezvous. This seagoing safari was offered only to that elite echelon of students who had successfully completed the first-year course in seamanship. About twenty boats signed up, eager as a kindergarten class on its way to the zoo.

Our destination was a lonely little harbor formed by a long sandspit that curved out from a narrow neck of deserted mainland. We were to meet there, drop anchor, lower the dinks, and hoist the cocktail flags.

Everything went according to plan. When we got there, the kids were zooming around the cove in the dinghies, a fire was blazing on the beach, the lobsters were in their pots, and the mariners were in their cups. Radios were blaring from every deck, and the flotilla was swinging at anchor—and I mean swinging.

It was real nice clambake. It would have lasted half the night but for a cold wind that suddenly sprang up and chilled everybody down to the last gin and tonic. By ten o'clock the party was over, and we all rowed back to our boats. Peace and quiet descended, and the Argonauts slumbered snugly in their foam-rubber bunks.

For a while, that is.

With no warning at all, a wild gust of wind ripped across the water, and the boats began to gyrate. My captain hit the deck before I had managed to open one eye. By the time I joined him, he was listening to the Coast Guard bulletins. The burden of their message was substantially this:

"Look, you clowns! Don't go out! If you're stupid enough to be out, go somewhere quick and stay put. If you'd bothered to check with us six hours ago, you'd know that a wind shift has put us in the direct path of Hurricane Helga's tail."

She must have been one Helga of a hurricane, because her tail was shimmying about forty knots an hour.

Now the fun really began. Mine enemy the anchor wasn't holding. We were faced with three possibilities. The wind could drive us right onto the sandspit and ground us. It could shift and blow us out to sea. Or it could swing us crashing into some other member of the armada. None of these choices seemed particularly appealing. We could see lights go on all over the harbor, and above the howl of the wind we heard engines revving up. The Power Squadron was stuck, but their anchors weren't.

I remembered all the lessons about the care and feeding of those beastly hooks. The mathematical equations, the scientific theorems. The ratios about tensile strengths and holding capacities. I thought about the formulas that postulate so many feet of chain per length and weight of vessel, the five to nine times scope per depth of water at low tide. Ha! Any woman knows you can't raise an anchor by the graph any more than you can raise a baby by the book. Comes a time when theory must give way to application. The time had arrived.

I assumed my battle station on the bow, planted my feet, in their nonskid shoes, firmly on the deck, and slid sprawling flat on my face. The boat pitched, the rain pelted down, and the order came from the bridge.

"Haul 'er up!"

Right then and there something snapped—my third lumbar vertebra and what remained of my sanity. I found myself addressing my opponent, the abominable anchor:

"Oh, thou hideous hook, harpy of a harpoon! This is war, you slimy pair of tongs—a tong war. Humble self will bend thy prongs over head of honorable husband. Send him to join venerable ancestors, ancient slave drivers for mighty pharaoh."

The commands kept issuing from headquarters.

"Let 'er go!"
"Pull 'er up!"
"Take in slack!"
"Pay out line!"
"Make 'er fast!"

My hands were raw, my back was in spasm, my mind was wandering.

"Haul 'er up, he says. Like 'Pass the butter.' What am I doing here? You have to be crazy. No, you have to have a husband who's crazy. A woman's place is in the home. Even the kitchen. The PTA. At her husband's side. Am I at his side? Not me! I'm fifteen feet in front of him, coping with you, you snake-fanged gaff, while he sits there pushing buttons!"

We went forward and backward and sideward. Sometimes I pulled up too soon. Sometimes too late. Sometimes I didn't make it at all. In between I stood guard with a boathook to fend off a hapless neighbor.

They say suffering clarifies the mind. I believe it, because a great truth was revealed to me that night. The whole thing is a conspiracy. It is man's revenge against woman for invading his salty little world.

How else to explain why men can split an atom and use it to send a submarine around the world; harness sonic beams to plumb the ocean depths; set an airfield afloat to land a battalion of planes. But they can't improve this antediluvian fork? They can't? They won't! May anchors everywhere rust away on the ocean's floor, and may barnacles feed on their pitted bones!

It was such pure, honest hatred that sustained me during that dark and dreary watch. That, and the righteous indignation that burned with a clear, white heat through the cold and starless hours that lagged behind the dawn. All in all, it was a witch's brew of a night, compounded of equal parts of cracked shin, skinned hands, and pulled tendons. Helga didn't give up till midmorning, and the open sea was still a bit sticky. We just didn't have the steam left to make it all the way home.

Then the skipper had such a brilliant idea, I forgave him everything. He decided to pull into a small landing about an hour away, where a friend had a summer cottage. We would tie up to his wharf, casually drop in on him, be coaxed to stay for lunch, and persuaded to spend the night. Next day, renewed and relaxed, we could start home.

The captain consulted his charts, plotted a careful course, and off we went. Not immediately, though. Naturally, the anchor decided this was the time to dig in, and I sacrificed my last fingernail getting it loose. But we made it, and an hour later, with journey's end in sight, I went below to that beautiful "stand-up head." Compared with the accommodations of the *Marlyn I,* this closet with a sink, hot water, and a mirror was luxury unparalleled. It provided a lovely interlude that lasted all of three minutes.

With a brutal crunch the *Marlyn II* came to a shuddering halt. I found myself tilted at a sixty-degree list, which is an extremely difficult angle at which to apply mascara. When I crawled topside, the captain's face was a study in horrified disbelief.

"We can't be on the rocks!" he kept saying. "The charts show plenty of water!"

Well, there it was again. The same old schism. Principle versus practice. In the days that followed, I did a little research. I found that the newest edition of *Chapman Piloting* devotes more than twenty full pages, replete with charts, diagrams, and formulas, to tides and currents. This arcane and scholarly exegesis winds up by advising the boatman that "the ultimate source of current information is your own eyesight and past experience." I also found that the *Encyclopaedia Britannica* devotes thirteen double-printed pages to the scientific data of tide calculations. It is filled with helpful hints like the following:

$$u = \frac{g}{a} H \cos\left(t - \frac{x}{c}\right) - \frac{1}{8}\frac{9^2 H^2}{c^3} \cos 2n \left(t - \frac{x}{c}\right) - \frac{3}{4} \frac{9^2 n H^2}{cH} \times \sin 2n \left(t - \frac{x}{3}\right)$$

There are dozens of these fine little ideas surrounded by a couple of hundred thousand explanatory words. And here's the kicker. The very last paragraph has this to say. And I quote it precisely:

"Of course, the irregular meteorological effects on sea level cannot be incorporated in a tide table, and hence any individual prediction is liable to differ considerably from the actual occurence."

Put that in your bos'n's pipe!

In other words, you make your guess and take your chances.

I also found that we'd run into one of those "irregular effects" known as neap tide. This is a condition that sometimes occurs after the first and third quarters of the moon when the high-water level stands at its lowest point. Which is a very good desciption of our emotional status at that moment.

Even these fascinating facts, had we known them, would have been cold comfort. The boat tottered on her keel, thumping her side against the bottom with sickening regularity. Each lurching blow was a stab in the heart. The Coast Guard finally came alongside and stayed till the water rose high enough to tow us off.

The captain stayed with his ship all the way to the nearest repair yard. The *Marlyn II* was a sadly battered boat. The most brutal damage had come from a jagged rock pounding away at our midships, right into my precious little bathroom. I can only ascribe it to hysteria, but I turned to my poor, bedeviled skipper and said:

"You know how I know that you're a real, genuine dedicated boatman? Because now it's fact, not theory. I can see with my own eyes, you actually have got rocks in your head!"

15 ❧ The Family That Sails Together...

Whenever it became necessary to plough the deep, troubled waters of fundamental concepts, the captain steered a course that veered palpably to starboard. On such matters we saw eye to eye. Take, for illustration, "The Importance of Being a Family." Even our thoughts on that subject were expressed in capital letters. Like "Viewing with Alarm the Erosion of the Cornerstone of the Judeo-Christian Ethic." Or "Lamenting the Fragmentation of the Basic Structure of Western Civilization." Also, "Rejecting Categorically the Illusory Values of a Permissive Society."

Or, as the captain put it, "I'll be Damned If I'm Going to Knock My Brains Out for a Group That Won't Buckle Down and Love Each Other!" We agreed that the family that plays together stays together, but we were at sword's point on how to go about it.

I am not implying that the argument, which was more procedural than substantive, "Threatened the Very Foundation of Our Marriage." But there did occur a few confrontations that sent the children scurrying for their security blankets. The captain insisted that boating was the solution. To begin with, he said, nowhere else could so many people live so constructively in so little space. Moreover, the hierarchical structure of command at sea was an object lesson in the obligations of power on the one hand and the respect due legitimate authority on the other.

I came up with several counterproposals. Camping, for instance. With consummate eloquence, I described the smell of cedar and balsam and wood smoke and bacon frying on a crisp morning. I talked about the joys of picking berries along a forest trail and the sheer magic of a bonfire under starlit skies. I pointed out that it was vital for children to relate to Mother Earth, to know her scents and sounds, her beauties and her bounties.

When all that failed to spark any enthusiasm, I suggested buying a farm. I exhorted him to consider that honest toil makes responsible citizens. That nurturing the soil and husbanding animals brings people close to the rhythms of nature and the miracle of life. He said that this was demonstrably impractical.

Then how about pursuing a sport in which we could all become champions? I recalled incredible circus acts, where four generations of a single family could be seen balancing on each other's noses, blindfolded, sixty feet above the cheering throngs. What literally kept them together? Discipline, that's what! Physical discipline! The family that trains together remains together. No?

Then let's acquire a small stable and master the techniques of the Spanish riding school. The family that rides together abides together. Thumbs down? Then what the hell would be wrong with studying music and learning four-part harmony? The family that sings together clings together.

It was conceded that these were reasonable ideas. There

was only one thing wrong with all of them: They were impossible to execute on a boat.

Thus, by a scrupulously fair process of elimination, the theater of operations was selected. The next step was coping with the logistics of the situation. My way of coping was to make out lists.

Somehow they always started with peanut butter. I don't know why. It may be simply that I was taking the coward's way out of the galley. But for many years peanut butter led all the rest. Then came thousands of essential items: Towels, tissues, Band-Aids, thermometers, sweaters, rubber pants, undershirts, animal crackers, plastic straws, stuffed elephants, crayons, coloring books, modeling clay, a pet turtle, a small library of Peter Rabbit, Bowser the Hound, Bugs Bunny and Scupper the Sea Dog, scissors, glue, colored paper, tinker toys, and building blocks.

It is all necessary because children are not merely miniature adults. They exist in a different dimension. They do not, for example, look upon wind, sun, and spray as positive pleasures. A small boat is to them not so much an escape as a method of confinement. And they are easily afflicted with a malady that necessitates frequent returns to shore. It is called cabin fever. The best way to effect a partial cure is to seek out the nearest cove or island, and having sighted such a haven, begin immediate preparations for a temporary layover.

First the anchor is lowered, and care is taken to see that it is absolutely secure. Next the dinghy is lowered, and care is taken to see that it does not capsize on the way down. Then the captain lowers himself and waits for the child who will be lowered as soon as he is ready.

That time comes when he is strapped into his life preserver, a mechanism he views with intense loathing, much as the average grown-up regards a straitjacket. The child is then lowered and is followed by a basket containing various necessaries: cookies, towels, face tissues, shovel and pail, iodine, and the like. Last the first mate lowers herself into the cockleshell.

Everybody can then go ashore and have a rousing good time throwing stones in the water, watching the boat to make sure the anchor is holding, or washing sand out of sneakers. After the festivities, they can all go back and repeat the initial procedure in reverse. Everything that goes down must eventually come up—including the aforementioned anchor.

Like the tides, the years flowed in and out, and their passing was reflected in my changing lists. Animal crackers gave way to hamburger buns; Peter Rabbit and Bowser the Hound were replaced by comic books; tinker toys abdicated in favor of water skis. Shore leave was more easily negotiated, and the children were occasionally remanded into their own custody. Sometimes the consequences were fascinating.

I remember a week we spent in a classy marina in Florida. This glorified parking lot was filled with hundreds of pleasure crafts, each one fit for Kublai Khan himself. It took great strength of character not to fall into a trough of greed, avarice, and sloth. But I cautioned myself. "Thou shall not covet thy neighbor's yacht. Nor the flunkies thereon." So I gathered up a mountain of laundry and prepared to lug it ashore. As I came topside, I saw our seven-year-old sitting alone on the aftdeck.

"I thought you were going with your father," I said.

"He went to the store. He didn't want to take me."

"I can understand his reluctance," I said. "You look terrible."

She was clad in torn blue jeans, a jelly-stained shirt, mismatched sox, and grimy sneakers.

"I have no clean clothes," she said. And fixed me with the steely eye of a tank commander.

"I'll give the steward a piece of my mind," I assured her.

"Can I go splore?"

"May I go explore," I corrected her automatically.

"That's what I said!"

"Yes, you may," I answered. "You have complete freedom. Only don't go farther than the end of this dock. You might get lost. Don't run on the docks. They're slippery. Don't fall in the water. It's dangerous. And don't poke your nose into the portholes of any other boat. It's bad form."

"That's zactly what you said yesterday," she replied.

"I apologize for boring you," I apologized.

When I returned from my ablutions, it was after noon, and she was nowhere to be seen. I was about to start a search party when she climbed aboard, looking more unkempt than ever.

"Where have you been?" I demanded. "You must be starving."

"Huh, uh." She shook her head. "I had my lunch."

"Where?"

"With a nice lady. She's my friend."

"She probably felt sorry for you. 'Poor, abandoned waif,' she must have thought, 'nobody cares.' What did you eat?"

"Rabbit. It was delicious."

"Rabbit? Who eats rabbit? Whom were you with, a couple of Florida crackers from the swamps?"

"We had toast with it. Not crackers."

"Where did she catch the rabbits? Under the wharves?"

"Don't be silly. It was a foreign rabbit."

"Imported, no less. What did it taste like?"

"Cheese. All melted and runny. I got some on my chin."

"Also on your shirt," I noted. "I'm beginning to understand. What you had was Welsh rarebit."

"That's what I said!"

Her forebearance was a direct rebuke.

"I'm going back to see her tomorrow."

"Now look, honey," I told her. "It was very nice of the lady, but you mustn't make a nuisance of yourself..."

"She invited me. She's very lonesome when she has no visitors, because she has no children and she isn't even married and she's going to show me how to broider. With colored thread."

"You mean embroider."

"That's what I said!"

It was all very nice. My mornings and part of the afternoons were all my own, and sometimes I even stretched out on the foredeck and invited a suntan. Just goes to prove, I thought, that there are some really lovely people in this world. Also that when you have none of your own, you have plenty of time to spend with other people's children. As I said to the captain:

"Some evening we must ask Myra Lynn's friend over here for dinner. The poor old lady must be dying for a little adult conversation."

One morning I asked my daughter, "What's your friend's name?"

"Agatha."

"How quaint. And what's the name of her boat?"

"*Mabel.* You know what we're going to do today?"

"What?"

"We're going to make necken."

"How do you do that?"

"How do I know until she shows me?"

She was charmingly patient.

"Well, what do you make them out of?"

"Flour and sugar and raisins and cimmamum and stuff like that."

"Oh, you mean schnecken."

"If you knew, why did you ask?"

"What do you do when Miss Agatha's busy? Sometimes she must be busy."

"She gives me things to make. Like I made a necklace out of beans. Agatha says kids need projects, 'cause the devil maketh work for ideal hands."

"For idle hands."

She opened her mouth, but I stopped her.

"I know. That's what you said."

After about five peaceful, lonesome mornings, I decided to introduce myself to Miss Agatha and invite her to dinner. A half-hour later, I was still looking for her. In that entire marina, there was no boat named Mabel. I trudged back to the office and made inquiries. My suspicions were confirmed. There was no boat registered named Mabel.

So I began a thorough check of every transom on that mile of docks. Some of the names made good reading. I saw *The His Not Hers, A Broad Aboard, The Sally Fourth, The Seasons, The Marrytime*. But no Mabel. Then I spotted her, sleek and shining, with flowered curtains drawn across her windows and geranium pots flanking her boarding ladder. She was called *Ma Belle*, and I should have known. Wasn't that what she said?

All was quiet as I stepped aboard and made my way forward along the narrow passageway skirting the cabin. There was my youngster on the foredeck, completely absorbed, bent over something in her lap. I stooped down to pat her head and stopped midway.

"What have you got there?" I hissed.

"Balloons."

She was surprised at my stupidity.

"Give them to me!" I said, "Give them to me at once!"

"They're mine!" she yelped.

"Not anymore," I said, and snatched them away from her.

She responded with a shriek of outraged indignation and sobs that would have melted a stone.

"What the hell's going on up there?" a voice from below-deck joined the chorus. "Didn't I tell you never to make any noise when I'm having visitors?"

Two seconds later, the owner of the voice was on deck, and I was face to face with Miss Agatha. It wasn't the face I'd been expecting. Cherry-red, bee-stung lips, Minnie Mouse eyelashes, long, yellow hair. And below them, the most buxom, bosomy curves ever seen through a filmy, hot pink peignoir. She was an eighteenth-century tavern wench out of Hogarth, and close behind her was her visitor, a rake who was making good progress.

"What's comin' off here?" Miss Agatha demanded.

"Your head, if you ever come near my child again!" I snarled. "How dare you give her these things to blow up?"

And I threw at her feet a box of the kind of balloons you can only get from your friendly neighborhood druggist.

"I don't know what you're so excited about!" Miss Agatha was frankly insulted. "What kinda girl do you think I am? I gave the kid a brand-new box that's never been used!"

"What's been used is my child!" I think I was screaming. "You used her to make this floating bordello look respectable!"

I gathered up my caterwauling child and disembarked. On the way out I kicked both of those domestic-looking geranium planters into the water. It was the least I could do for Madame Agatha.

The ensuing ten minutes were rough. My fervent assurances that I was not against balloons were somehow unconvincing.

"I do not hate balloons," I insisted. "I like most balloons. Some of my best friends are balloon blowers."

"Then why . . . ?"

"Because those particular balloons weren't clean. This is a matter of hygiene, not antiballoonism."

"Ha!"

She looked at me like a prosecuting attorney who has just trapped a hostile witness.

"That's reedickalus! My balloons were so new they came wrapped in separate little envelopes!"

"Ridiculous," I amended.

"See?" She was triumphant. "That's just what I said!"

16 ⚘ The Sea Is Full of Surprises

We never again enjoyed a marine hostelry as elegant as that one in Florida. They just didn't come like that along the shores of Long Island Sound. But our native waters did provide several major facilities for the entertainment of growing children. Fishing, for one thing.

The captain and I invested in rods and reels, all kinds of tackle, and compartmented steel boxes to keep them in. We built a zinc-lined receptacle the size of a bathtub, with a hinged lid, in which to stow our catch. We also bought bait, which came packed in nasty little cardboard cartons that leaked copiously five minutes after purchase.

This bait was material from which horror movies are made. It consisted of two hell-spawned creatures called night crawlers and bloodworms. They looked like their names. One is a slimy, gray, dripping earthworm that emerges from its burrow only in the dark of night. Even that is too often. The other is an ensanguined, gory thing that spurts and bleeds when impaled on a hook. Completely traumatic to me was the sight of a soggy box in the refrigerator, half filled with leftover bait, nestling next to leftover roast beef and apple pie. It was my inflexible contention that any fish that would feed upon such stuff was obviously not fit to eat.

Take a flounder, if you're able to. This fish is almost one dimensional, flat, flabby, and sickly white. It wears its two eyes on the same side of its head and looks for all the world like a fish designed by Picasso in an unthinking moment. Or, let us consider the eel. This mephitic monster brings up with it from the primordial ooze a stench so overpowering that I never allowed one aboard. If an eel had the temerity to hook itself on our bait, I gave orders that the hook, line, and sinker were to be cut away and consigned to the depths from whence they came.

Once we pulled up one specimen that defied the laws of probability and boggled the mind. The thing had the body of a fish, a head like a rodent, four rudimentary orange-colored legs, and mothlike wings on its back. When it landed on the deck, it tried to propel itself along on those primitive pedicles.

Marlo Junior, whose capacity for intellectual inquiry was boundless, thought it might be the piscatorial missing link between sea and land animals. Nothing would do but that we haul it down to the ichthyology department of the Museum of National History and get a professional opinion. I was all for throwing it back and wiping the experience from memory, but I was outvoted as usual, so we put the thing into a bucket of seawater, along with a few bloodworms to keep it company, stashed it in the back of the car, and sloshed our way twenty-five miles into the city.

Expert opinion there labeled it a flying gurnard. I called it a walking horror and offered to donate it to the museum. Marlo Junior had a different plan. An ardent ecologist long before the word was discovered by the relevant faddists, he insisted we take the thing back to its native habitat. He had no intention of interfering in any way with the evolutionary processes of nature. What persuaded me to do things his way was the positive malignancy in the ratlike eyes of the thing as it stared balefully up from the bucket. To pursue any other course was to court malediction.

We carried the pail back to the car, which was beginning to smell like a garbage scow, and transported the thing back to Long Island Sound, where, I trust, it is alive and well and somehow justifying its existence.

As time went on, our children brought their little friends aboard for long, fun-filled holidays. Their parents evidently approved of our way of life and were glad to have their youngsters join us. They themselves were unhappily unable to provide our kind of healthy, family diversion, as they were busy in the clubhouses, bars, and golf courses of upper suburbia. To keep the moppets occupied, we built an elaborate teak landing platform on the rear of our boat about a foot above the waterline. From this sturdy perch they could dive and swim or float on life preservers from morning till night.

Swimming from a boat, way out in the open water, was a thrill and an adventure for most children—but not for all. Marlo Junior would have no part of it.

"How do you know what's down there?" he asked. "There might be sharks. Sharks live in seawater. They inhabit the whole world of oceans."

His reasoning was perfectly logical and consistent with his entire outlook. From his first sentient moment he had looked at this earth with judicious eyes and tempered his appraisal with conservative evaluations. No wonder that little boy grew up to read Aristotle for pleasure and hung a life-size picture of William Buckley, Jr., on his wall in college. He accepted fantasy on its own terms and never confused it with reality. To him, sharks were the ultimate reality of mindless voracity and insatiable rapacity. Thus it was ill advised to go swimming.

To his father and me it was sad and disappointing to watch all the other ecstatic aquanauts romp and roister while he sat patiently on the sidelines. So we set about allaying his suspicions. There were no sharks in the Sound, we assured him. In the tropic waters of Florida, in the South Seas, out in the open oceans. That's where they were.

We coaxed him. We urged him. We pleaded with him. And finally, because he trusted our infinite wisdom, he believed us. The great day finally came when Marlo Junior joined the others and outswam them all. The captain and I congratulated ourselves.

About a month later, at the end of a glorious afternoon, we hauled anchor and headed in for a shore dinner at a pretty little fishing town on the north shore of the Sound. The children were allowed to go ashore first and wait for us. Just as we were leaving the boat, we heard frantic footsteps pounding along the wharf. It was Marlo Junior, pale and visibly shaken.

"Go up there and see what's hanging at the boathouse!" he panted. "Just go up there and see!" And he looked at us with stricken and accusing eyes.

With a headlong rush, he jumped into the *Marlyn* and slammed the cabin door. The captain and I took off along the dock and stopped only when we ran into a crowd of people clustered at the end of the pier. Then we saw what they were looking at and stood speechless and transfixed.

Two enormous gray sharks, hoisted by their tails, hung ominously from a scaffold. Their gaping maws, stretched in hellish grins, glistened with rows of dagger teeth. We turned to an old fisherman who seemed to have a proprietary interest in those obscene creatures.

"Where did they come from?" we gasped.

"Right outside the harbor, ma'am. Guess all the garbage

from the yachts is what's bringin' 'em in. Nasty lookin' brutes, ain't they?"

No amount of persuasion could induce our disillusioned child to join us for dinner. Had it not been for the rest of the troops, his father and I would have foresworn it, too. I may say that it was a singularly joyless occasion. How do you restore faith once traduced? How do you plead ignorance, having proclaimed knowledge? We castigated ourselves unnecessarily. Marlo Junior met us on the dock when we returned.

"Look," he said, "Don't worry about it. I know you didn't lie to me."

He almost smiled.

"I figured it out. There's a difference between the truth and honesty. They're not the same thing at all!"

I have thought about that bit of profound wisdom many times since.

Children have a habit of growing on you, too. There came a time when they couldn't be expected to join us just as a matter of course. There were other things to do. Basketball games and sweet-sixteen parties, and football rallies, and movie dates.

I remember one weekend when they bowed out at the last minute because of some pressing social commitments. The captain and I set out without them. It was a beautiful day, blue skies, smooth seas, and a gentle breeze to temper the sun. But I noticed the captain sitting at the wheel, somehow not his usual self. There was a shadow on his face and a slump upon his shoulders. He was strangely quiescent, and the regular barrage of orders and directives were not forthcoming.

"What's the matter?" I asked, as if I didn't know.

He shrugged and managed to look put upon, chagrined, and morose, all at the same time.

"Now hear this!" I admonished him. "Never let it be said

that the family that sails together fails together! Wherever they are, and whatever they're doing, remember, they're well armed, well taught, and well intentioned. And they got that way through no accident."

I went below and left him to think about it. In a few minutes I heard his yell.

"Haul the anchor. We're going up to Mystic. Also, you forgot to bring in the bumpers. And make some ice tea, will you? It's hot up here!"

Everything was normal again. Captain Bligh was back, shouting orders from the bridge.

17 ⁊⁊ Status Afflatus

It is generally believed that there exists a benevolent fraternity among seafarers—a kinship born of common passions and pursuits and perils. There is a large measure of truth in this conviction. The brotherhood of boatmen becomes heart-warmingly visible when disaster strikes or tragedy threatens. Then people perform generously, selflessly, and heroically on behalf of others who face danger on the water.

BUT!! When no emergency looms, and all things are busy being equal, then nothing is equal! Status and position and one-upmanship can be found doing business as usual. The snob mob is ubiquitous and, land or sea, it's the same cock-eyed world. Every arena has its own status requirements, though the formulas for exclusivity and permissible hauteur are often shrouded in mystery. It is not unreasonable to postulate the existence, somewhere in the primordial bush, of a tribe that thumbs its collective nose—ring and all—at all neighboring clans . . . its aristocracy firmly rooted in a few remote ancestors who caught, speared, cooked, and ate more missionaries than all the other aborigines. The rationale of status securement boggles the mind and may well turn the stomach. In boating society, status is compounded of three major elements: 1) size of vessel; 2) presence of a professional crew; 3) membership in a hubris-happy yacht club.

According to Chapman, a boat gets to be a yacht when it reaches sixty-five feet.* According to custom, its owner reaches social respectability when he takes unto himself a real, honest-to-God captain. Then, armed with proof of correct forebears, desirable affiliations, and plenty of money, he can join the right club and become a proper yachtsman.

Over the years, the captain and I made quite a few incursions into the fast sea-lanes of the yacht club set. The belle monde seemed to do a lot of drinking. I venture to say that many of them ran some pretty tight ships. Among that group we had two very dear friends, John and Elena Gaunt. A first impression might suggest that ours was a one-sided relationship, as the Gaunts had never set foot on our boat and we were forever wining and dining on theirs. Nonetheless, the friendship was of mutual design. John and Ellie Gaunt liked having "interesting people" around so they could show them off to other "interesting people." They themselves had very little to say, so they collected inhabitants of more exotic, gossipy milieus. For instance, they embraced embassy personnel (preferably British), foreign correspondents (preferably *The New York Times*), authors (preferably of best sellers), and show business folk (any kind would do). That's where we came in. At least that's where Marlo came in. He was connected, therefore, collected.

* The British call any sail-equipped pleasure craft sixteen feet and over a "yacht." They also call private schools "public" schools. But as they have enjoyed a longer history of maritime enterprise than we, and practiced the intricacies of caste systems more effectively, I will not quarrel with their right to their own definitions.

As for us, you had only to see their yacht to understand the Gaunts attraction for us. The *Gauntlet* was unique. Originally built by the navy as an experimental pursuit craft, she had triple screws, ninety-two feet at the waterline, a canoe-shaped stern, and a cruising speed of almost forty knots. She had no beam to speak of—just long, lovely lines, sleek and narrow from stem to stern. (Come to think of it, that's a pretty fair description of its owner's wife.) Bought and converted into a pleasure yacht by John Gaunt, she was still the fastest thing of her size afloat. Even her name fit like a glove. The *Gauntlet* was a flippant challenge flung at every other powerboat on Long Island Sound.

A day aboard the *Gauntlet* was a wallow in luxury. The gulf that separates "boating" and "yachting"was immediately apparent. Take the ketchup and the mustard, for instance. They came to the table in their own silver filigree bottle holders. Service was unending, with a captain, a steward, and an Oriental houseboy in attendance. The most one had to do for one's self was acquire a suntan, and even that was made easy. Tanning lotion, lounging pads, cold drinks, and chilled fruit were brought to the foredeck. It was not considered good form to spit grape seeds to windward, however, and one had to be careful. But then nothing is perfect.

Except Ellie Gaunt. Just to look at her was a privilege. Her clothes, which she changed every watch, never wrinkled. Fabric hung on her willow-wand frame the way a cobweb clings to a flower, with no vulgar pressure from bosom, belly, or backside. Any pressure exerted came from the inner woman and was apt to be felt by her husband, her crew, and occasionally her guests. I once made the mistake of sitting on an antique satin bunk spread in a damp bathing suit. Only once, believe me. Ellie, as she was wont to tell you, was a perfectionist.

Her most avowedly perfect possession was Cappy Yar.

(*Cappy* short for captain, *Yar* short for Yarborough.) Cappy was the very model of a seagoing English gentleman. Tall, spare, neat, and nautical, he had a pipe perpetually clenched in his even white teeth and little sun-etched lines running from his steady blue eyes. As he stood behind the wheel in his starched khakis, you just knew he had plenty of starch in his character, too. Ellie was forever talking about him. Once she said to me, "I haven't told you the latest story about Cappy, have I, darling?"

"No," I answered. "And I can't thank you enough."

That was misplaced levity, and it was followed by a brief lecture.

"Not having a skipper of your own, dear one," she admonished, "you cannot imagine how rare a find he is."

"That is true," I admitted.

"My friends at the club are green with envy! You don't know what goes on at that club!"

"That is even truer," I agreed.

"Most captains," she went on, "are liars, thieves, alcoholics, and not above blackmail now and then. Seeing as how other women's husbands when they're out fishing with the boys are not, strictly speaking, out with the boys . . ."

Moreover, unlike a lot of skippers who take kickbacks from purveyors of everything from bait to booze, Cappy saved them a lot of money. At the end of every season, she told me, Cappy ran the *Gauntlet* down to Florida and put her up at an out-of-the-way, not too plushy boatyard. There he overhauled her and got ready to meet John and Ellie when they arrived in Palm Beach for their short winter vacation. Dockage would be arranged at a posh yacht club, and when they left, Cappy would simply take the boat down the inland waterway to the low-rent marina and spend the rest of the winter saving money for his grateful employers.

My own captain spent the winter at home, waiting for the

boat show to come to town. This annual event was the one true harbinger of spring, and every year we went to see it. Always we managed to find some new gadget that was guaranteed to make life on the bounding main better than before. The particular year I'm thinking of was no exception. We came across a terrific new item—a shiny new forty-two-foot cabin cruiser. I was moved to ask one simple question before he signed his name to a bill of sale.

"Do you think," I asked, "do you suppose that possibly we are being influenced by anybody ... Or by anything anybody may own?"

"Absolutely not!" said the boat's future captain. "It's just that you deserve something bigger, and better, and more beautiful!"

You cannot argue with the truth, so I conceded the point and began to dream about color schemes for the *Marlyn IV* and how to make her more beautiful than her predecessors.

She exceeded my dreams. She was a knockout and I couldn't wait for Ellie and John to see her. When they finally paid us a visit, we showed them everything and saved the master stateroom for last. Ellie inspected the tiled shower, the real beds, the rug on top of the carpet. In a reflex gesture, she ran a rosy-tipped finger along the edge of the mirrored dressing table. Finding no trace of salt or silt, she smiled approvingly.

"It's very nice, angel," she said. "Plenty of closet room ... You've thought of almost everything."

"Plenty of locker room," I amended automatically. "And what did I forget?"

"At least one closet with a combination lock on it, and a little safe in the back of it built into the wall."

"Into the bulkhead," I said. "And whatever for?"

"For when you're away on a weekend and you want to go ashore for some casual lunch or something, and you don't want to wear your good jewelry." She was being very patient. "Where are you going to put it?"

"Good heavens," I said. "Is there no end to the problems one faces at sea? Dear one," I continued through clenched teeth, "don't you know that nobody—but nobody—brings real jewels aboard anymore! That's simply looking for trouble. Do what I do . . . have your good pieces copied and leave the real ones at home."

I was tempted to suggest another place she could stow her precious baubles. But I merely consigned Ellie, her exquisite condescensions, and her trinkets to a very capacious and burglar-proof locker—the one belonging to Davy Jones.

The following winter, instead of putting the *Marlyn IV* in dry dock, we took her to Florida. We tied up at a modest little marina located somewhere between Miami and Palm Beach. The rates were low, and all the necessary amenities were at hand: a Laundromat, clean showers, a grocery store. Best of all there was an unpretentious dockside restaurant that served the best Italian food west of Palermo. Reputed to be owned by a group of entrepreneurs who liked to keep a low profile while engaging in high finance, the place boasted a great cook who had been imported from Sicily. As the old man who tended the gas pumps told me, "Outside, shesa dump. But inside, shesa great!"

One evening before dinner, the captain and I took a stroll along the rickety piers, trying to peer into the more interesting boats along the way. Suddenly we stopped. There, at the end of the longest wharf, rode the *Gauntlet*, ebony hull gleaming in the sunset, a swan among geese, a princess among peasants. No one was aboard, so we betook ourselves up to the restaurant to question Enzo, the waiter. Enzo the Enforcer, we called him, because he looked like the gorilla that stood behind Edward G. Robinson or Jimmie Cagney in a gangster movie made in the late forties.

"Enzo," queried Marlo, "you know that big black boat out there? We stopped by, but nobody's aboard. Where's her captain?"

"Cap'n Yar?" Enzo shrugged. "He's prolly somewheres on a business trip."

"On a business trip?" Marlo repeated. "What other kind of business is he in?"

The Enforcer looked surprised at our ignorance.

"You name it, he's in it," he said. He pointed out the window. "See them stores on the docks? The gas pumps and everything . . . ?" He shook his head in admiration. "They're all Cappy's. Also that motel across the street, and the mobile home park down at the Keys . . . lots of stuff."

"No kidding!" I breathed. "Captain Yar must be very rich!"

"So's you'd be if you was to own a ship like that one. That's one helluva boat—buhlieve me."

"You've been on it?" Marlo asked. "You've been on the *Gauntlet?*"

"Yeah. Once when the boss was entertainin' some guys from Vegas and the reg'lar waiter took sick. What a party! Good thing we was three miles out."

"You mean that boat's for charter?" I demanded.

"Sure, if you can come up with big bucks. Set ya back about two grand a day. When you think about all those classy dames he's got in the stable, and the service 'n all, Cappy's gotta get top dollar. Betcha in season he rakes in fifteen thou a week."

"Wonderful!" said Marlo with a very straight face.

"Wonderful!" I echoed. "It is a very gracious way to entertain."

Outside the restaurant I gave way to shock.

"How can Cappy take a chance like that?" I dithered. "What makes him think he can get away with it?"

"Get away with what?"

I noticed Marlo was grinning from ear to ear. "Get away with running the fanciest floating casino and cat house on southern waters," I hissed.

"Honey," said the captain. "Calm down ... hasn't it occurred to you that Cappy knows exactly what he's doing, because the owner of the *Gauntlet* might just be a senior partner in the enterprise?"

"Mama mia." For a minute I was speechless. Then I said, "What about Ellie and her Baccarat crystal and Imari china and Porthault linen?"

"What she doesn't know won't bother her," the captain assured me.

"And what's more, nothing is irreplaceable."

"Except Cappy!" I chortled. "Cappy is irreplaceable. Ellie told me so."

"Right," he said. "He is an exception."

And so, I'm happy to say, are all the status-seeking, label-loving members of the elite fleet. They are, thank God, a minority. Most boating people are a generous, sturdy, down-to-earth breed who know what's important. To smell the sea and taste the spray. To feel the sun and the wind. To hear the swish of water under your keel. To see the colors change in the sky. And to be aware of the wonder of it all.

18 ∾ Before You Jump Off the Deep End

Suppose we disregard all the dangers and discomforts, the unending work and frustrations to which a boat owner subjects himself. To perceive his lemminglike instinct for self-destruction, one need follow him no farther than his own boatyard.

A boatyard is a triumph of unorganized chaos, uncollected debris, and uncompromising prices. It is a large, outdoor waiting room. The customer waits for his boat to be put into the water in the spring, hauled out of the water in the fall, and serviced the rest of the time. The docks wait to be repaired. The garbage waits to be collected. The owner of the yard waits to be paid. He is the only one who doesn't have to wait long, because there are plenty of would-be customers waiting for the privilege of using his facilities at any price.

The steady undercurrent of noise you hear at one of these marinas, apart from the ring of hard cash on the barrelhead, is the chorus of groans and whimpering of boatmen at bay. There is always something they need, be it service, repair, or equipment. And at a boatyard it is strictly a seller's market. There are simply too many boats for the existing shoreline.

These dockside depots are quite a bit like the old-fashioned, company-owned coal towns. They own the general store, the vending machines, the gas pumps, the carpenter, machine and paint shops, and the equipment-supply franchises. If you are lucky enough to find somebody to do work for you elsewhere, he is honor bound to tack 10 percent on your bill for the home-base operator. If you discover an artisan who can do a job quicker, better, or cheaper, you can't avail yourself of his talents. Outside labor is forbidden at all boatyards on pain of excommunication. Life in these autocracies is further complicated by the shorthandedness of the personnel. The sight of one painter, one carpenter, and one mechanic trying to ready forty boats in two weeks is a classic illustration of the law of supply and demand. It explains why two coats of paint on a thirty-foot vessel costs more than Michelangelo was paid for the entire ceiling of the Sistine Chapel.

The attitude of these boat boutiques is consistent and predictable. It is the character of its customers that suffers a drastic change. A calm, rational man is apt to become a complaining hysteric. A pleasant, easygoing individual becomes a hostile paranoiac.

A typical case was our dockside neighbor. Seldom have I known a more soft-spoken, peace-loving husband and father. The doting parent of four children, ranging in age from three to ten, he wanted to share his love for the sea with his family. After one season aboard a little outboard motorboat, his wife had had it. She laid down the law. Either they bought a bigger boat with bathroom facilities or he could take to the bounding main all by himself. So he came to our pirate's den and paid more than he could afford for a craft with indoor plumbing. Things went fine the first week. Then something went wrong with the disposal system.

He did the logical thing. He took his problem to Mr. Mac-Goniff, the boatyard owner. After a cursory inspection, he was informed that a vital part was broken, but with a little patience he could expect repairs within a few days, just as soon as the contraption could be flown in from Kalamazoo. The days stretched into weeks, and half of the summer was gone. The bathroom remained inoperable. Our friend pleaded, demanded, threatened. The management blamed the airlines, the factory, the labor unions, and the general breakdown of national morale.

We used to see the poor fellow, standing wistfully alone at the dock, watching other happy families sail off for their weekend excursions. His wife kept her word and stayed home with the children. The trusting man didn't realize that Mac-Goniff's Marina was so happily engaged in running up big bills for big boats that it had no intention of wasting manpower on his picayune problem. Finally, Black Beard himself took time to offer a temporary solution.

"Go up to my store," he said, "and buy a couple of plastic buckets with screw-on lids."

Seafaring men, he intimated, from Sir Francis Drake to Admiral Dewey, had done pretty well with less.

Embarrassed but desperate, our friend explained his plight to a clerk at the store, who was very understanding. Not only did he analyze the mechanical breakdown, but he told our friend how to fix it. He explained that this was such a common situation that the store carried an unlimited supply of those essential parts if ever the problem occurred again. Our friend stood for a moment in grim silence. Then he bought the little gismo and the bucket, too.

The next morning he herded his whole family aboard and promised to repair the plumbing the next day. In the meantime, he told them to rough it and demonstrated the use of the plastic pail. That evening, when they got back to shore, he strode up to the yard office armed with his interim convenience. Standing in front of MacGoniff, who was seated at his desk preparing the monthly statements, this once-meek man unscrewed the lid of his bucket.

"Never mind fixing my head," he said softly. "I'm going to fix yours!"

And he upended the container exactly where he thought it would do the most good. In honor of this man's protest, I dedicate the following poem:

Song of the Sucker

B is for the Bank account you plundered
O is what I Owe you every day
A is for the Assets you have sundered
T is for the Triple Time I pay!
Y is for the Years that you have soaked us
A is for Accounts forever due
R is for the Rates that nearly choked us
D is for the Debts forever new!
Put them all together
They spell BOATYARD
Two words that mean just plain screw you!

Boating fever is highly contagious and is rapidly becoming endemic to this country. It is difficult to prevent and almost impossible to cure. You would do well to be able to recognize the symptoms so that if it should strike your family, you will be prepared to cope with the situation. Briefly, they are as follows: buying; improving; garnishing; comparing; outgrowing; selling; and trading up.

If you commit to memory the first letters of each successive stage of the syndrome, you will at least be forewarned as to general prognosis. Try to remember B-I-G-C-O-S-T, and then take the necessary steps. Let us examine them one by one, as they develop in the patient.

CONFESSIONS OF A BOAT LOVER'S WIFE

First: He *buys* a boat. Because it's just what he has always wanted. It fits his needs, his purse, his dreams. He loves her.

Second: He *improves* her. He adds certain necessities. Because he needs them. The boat needs them. The family's safety requires them. He loves her even more.

Third: He *garnishes* her. He adds things because they make her more beautiful, more luxurious, more comfortable. Now she's perfect. And he adores her!

Then: He *compares* her—to another boat. One he's seen at the boat show. Or at the next dock. Or anywhere. He begins to doubt her.

And: He realizes he's *outgrown* her. She's inadequate. He's progressed as a seaman and needs more in a boat. More power. More seaworthiness. More room. He's disappointed in her.

So: He *sells* her. She's great for beginners. But not for him or his family. Or his guests. He can't do anything more for her. Or with her.

Therefore: He *trades* up. He gets a bigger boat. With greater comfort, more space, more everything—including expense. But she's worth it. She's just what he has always wanted. She fits his needs, his purse, his dreams. He loves her.

Like malaria, boating fever is cyclic and recurrent. It takes patience, tact, and understanding on the part of the victim's loved ones. There are times when he will go hot and cold trying to choose between diesels because they are safer, and gas engines because they are cheaper. He may be convulsed by the choice between a planing hull because it's faster and a round one because it's smoother. He may suffer sleepless nights thinking about fiberglass versus teak, sail versus power, chrome versus steel. The thought to hold fast to, however, is the hopeful fact that the disease, though lingering, is never fatal.

We have lived through it, the captain and I, and have acquired in the process a measure of immunity. We are no longer susceptible to the ravages of the boatman's malady. Our recovery was complete, I realized, when we built our forty-five foot, air-conditioned cabin cruiser, the *Marlyn V*. She took a lot of planning, a lot of hardheaded thinking, and she benefited by our fifteen-year record of mistakes, inexperience, and delusions of grandeur. We have owned her now for six months.

We love her flying bridge, her commodious salon, her ample bathroom facilities. She is a wonderful boat! All she needs, really, the captain says, is an automatic pilot, a stabilizer, and a little auxiliary outboard motor dinghy. And it seems to me that the engines are really a little bit underpowered.

Epi Log

So how do we explain the whole funny business of boating? Is there some basic reason for this strange love affair with the sea? Could it be just one more fad of the restless American? Or merely the pursuit of status. Or sheer escape. Or a simple rebellion against an automated age.

Truth is an elusive lady. Just when we think we have her cornered, she's apt to slip right through our fingers. But I think I caught a glimpse of her not long ago on a quiet street a thousand miles from the nearest ocean.

It was one of those golden days when the earth drouses in the heat of midsummer ... when dreams possess the very young and nostalgia invades the rest of us. I saw a very little boy sitting on a curb, his bare feet dangling in the road. Above his head an old maple stretched its branches and dappled his tousled hair with sunlight. In his right hand he held a homemade fishing pole and at his side was a little toy boat. Every now and then he lifted his rod to make sure no monster had stolen his bait. And every now and then his free hand would reach out and pat his boat, just to tell her that they were still together.

I watched him for a long time. He never saw me. How could he? He was a grown-up man, in his own brave boat, somewhere far at sea. And his eyes were fixed on his own wonderful, wide horizon.